Brief Li

E.M. Forster

Brief Lives:
E.M. Forster

Richard Canning

ET REMOTISSIMA PROPE

Brief Lives
Published by Hesperus Press Limited
4 Rickett Street, London SW6 1RU
www.hesperuspress.com

First published by Hesperus Press Limited, 2009

Designed and typeset by Fraser Muggeridge studio
Printed in Jordan by Jordan National Press

ISBN: 978-1-84391-916-2

Contents

Childhood and Cambridge, 1879–1901

Edward Morgan Forster – 'Morgan' to all – was born on New Year's Day 1879 at his parents' home, 6 Melcombe Place, Dorset Square, London. When he was but twenty-two months old, Forster lost his father to tuberculosis, the curse of the Forsters. He would consequently be brought up entirely by women. His boyhood, he remembered, had been 'a haze of old ladies'. May Wyld, a childhood friend, thought Forster was treated 'like a piece of Dresden china'; 'cossetted [sic] all his life'. If true, as seems likely, this was because of his mother. Alice Clara – 'Lily', of sturdier stock than her husband, would live into her nineties and was by some way the most important woman in her son's life.

Lily was born into a solid middle-class family named Whichelo (plausibly a corruption of the French 'Richelieu'). Her many sisters – Georgiana, Mary Eleanor, Rosalie – made up many of Forster's 'ladies'. Her father, a teacher, died young, in 1867, leaving her mother Louisa with ten children and no income. Louisa took in lodgers and placed her children in the only respectable positions available. Her daughters became governesses; her sons clerks. Lily – nicknamed 'the ready beast' for her answering back – was the exception. Mr Tayloe, the family doctor, took her to visit one Marianne Thornton, unmarried member of a prosperous South London family. Then seventy, she lived with her niece, Henrietta Synnot, not in the great family house – 'Battersea Rise', overlooking Clapham Common – but in 'East Side' nearby. Both ladies took to the young Lily, and she was adopted.

Henrietta first organised Lily's education, until Marianne – 'Aunt Monie' to Forster – arranged for her to study in Brighton. In turn she became a governess, with Monie securing several positions. The last was with a Mrs Farrer, an old friend now living in Abinger Hall, Surrey. Lily stayed there many years; it was Morgan's childhood home. Meanwhile, however, Monie's nephew Edward Morgan Llewellyn Forster began courting Lily. Forster's father was the son of an Irish clergyman, Charles Forster, and Laura Thornton, daughter of the well-off Henry, one of the so-called 'Clapham Sect' of religious free-thinkers, intellectuals and philanthropists. Edward had been well educated – at Charterhouse, and Trinity, Cambridge – and was beginning a career in architecture.

The couple married in early 1877 and moved to Melcombe Square, near Marylebone Station in London. Lily was pregnant by December, but lost this child in childbirth. Forster arrived on 1st January 1879; his christening took place in Holy Trinity Church, Clapham Common. Henrietta was godmother. The baby was already registered under the name his parents had chosen, Henry Morgan. However, when the verger asked for his name, Forster's father was not paying attention, and gave his own. Thus the future novelist became victim of his first 'muddle', and remained Edward Morgan Forster, like his father. Since his father died before Forster's second birthday, he had no memories of him, and never sought to discover more. His mother expressed disappointment in her former husband; that presumably sufficed. Forster wrote an entire book on Marianne Thornton, but only glanced at his father, 'always... remote to me. I have never seen myself in him, and the letters from him and the photographs of him have not helped.' Drawings made by Edward on holidays in France and Italy reveal a talented draughtsman. Photographs suggest a good-humoured, perhaps raffish personality.

In 1883, Lily and her son moved to Stevenage, Hertfordshire, after a period staying with friends. The house Lily rented, 'Rooksnest', was a mile and a half from the station, though enchantingly rural; it would inspire the setting of *Howards End*. She was worried about Morgan's health, convincing herself the boy would not thrive in bad city air. Still, they frequently guested at East Side, though Henrietta later somewhat resented their popularity with Monie.

Morgan, a precocious little boy, soon earned the nickname 'The Important One'. Monie noted, positively, his 'intense enjoyment of the world', but warned of his 'proportionate misery when anything is withheld from him'. Lily called him 'Poppy', a nickname he used in letters to her throughout adulthood (as well as 'Pop Snake', 'Clever Clogs', 'Machiavelli Clogs' and even 'Fred'). On one occasion, aged four, he refused to socialise with the adults, telling his nurse, 'Can't you tell the people I am busy reading?' At five he was writing his own tales, 'long stories that have never happened except inside my head'. Monie encouraged Lily to dress Morgan according to the fashion – in girlish garments – and to keep his hair long. He resembled Little Lord Fauntleroy.

Lily could only deal with the intense expression of his desires by spoiling her son, since 'we have rather a life of it if we do anything baby doesn't like,' as she informed Monie. Morgan played with dolls, including one favourite, Sailor Dollar, about whom he wove complex histories of derring-do. Combat, though, would never appeal. Morgan longed to be cowardly, not brave, he told Lily, since 'people hurt you when you are brave.' Furbank described their relationship as nothing less than a 'love-affair'. It certainly accommodated some unusual conduct, such as Lily, aged twenty-nine, letting her hair down and pretending to be a girl of fifteen to her five-year-old son. One day, Morgan pledged only ever to marry her, and was disconsolate when told, 'Boys can't marry their mothers.'

Forster's early friendships were either with maids or the garden labourers at Rooksnest. One, Ansell, 'a snub-nosed, pallid, even-tempered youth', provided a character's name in *The Longest Journey.* He and Morgan were allowed to play on Wednesday afternoons. Forster read aloud from *The Swiss Family Robinson*, and taught Ansell arithmetic. The boy, Forster later revealed, 'probably did more than anyone towards armouring me against life'. His aunts and uncles were frequent visitors. Morgan adored talkative Rosie, who alone dared to customise his name so it resembled hers: 'Morgie'. Louisa Whichelo, his grandmother, also inspired him. She claimed to dislike all women and their ways – a position he effectively inherited – arguing, 'I'm not a woman, so I must be a mule.'

Several tutors visited Rooksnest until Forster reached eleven. His rather idyllic childhood then ended abruptly. Morgan was sent to Kent House, a preparatory school in Eastbourne. Nick-named 'Mousie', he was soon bullied for his gentleness; he struck his peers as a mother's boy. One letter home complains that they were 'looking over the letter while I write'. He took up a range of unexceptional hobbies: stamp-collecting; keeping pets, such as a rabbit, and fish in an aquarium. He had a passion for drawing, played the triangle in school concerts, and read avidly. By the time he was almost ten, Forster was spreading his passion for books, selecting George Eliot's *Scenes of Clerical Life* as Lily's Christmas present.

He received practically no introduction to the facts of life. Forster later admitted he had first understood sex aged thirty – that is, after publishing his first three novels. Lily had taught him his penis was 'dirty'. At school, it was described by others as 'a beastly little brown thing'. An essay entitled 'Sex' reveals that Forster grew up thinking his penis would melt in the bath if the prepuce were drawn back. He knew he had long 'felt deeply about boys in books'. But he did not connect this to anything sexual until he was seduced, aged twelve, by a middle-aged man whilst out walking. According to 'Sex', the confused young Forster obliged the man by masturbating him to climax. Afterwards, the stranger offered him a shilling tip, which was greeted by a very Forsterian refusal. He informed the headmaster, but the offender was never caught. Morgan must have been traumatised. That day, he wrote only the word 'Nothing' for his diary entry.

He wrote and received letters constantly ('I have letters pouring in from every side'); to Lily, to Louisa and to Louisa's friend Maimie Aylward. Only to his mother was his unhappiness revealed. The litany had begun after the first week of school: 'I think I will tell you I am not happy.' Other letters lingered on minor abuses at the hands of boys and teachers. One schoolmaster 'came in and tried to be funny, pinching me under the bedclothes'. He had dropped Forster's book on him, although 'the swelling and the bruise have [now] gone down very much.' A half-century later, a comic essay on rationing, 'You Sausage!' (1941), began with an evocation of the playground name-calling. Still, 'to be called a sausage was not an irreparable social disaster for a little boy, and sometimes, by assuming a jollity which I was far from feeling, I succeeded in diverting my persecutors to some other target. "They do not really like me," I thought, "still they are not quite sure about me."' Morgan befriended one boy, Henson, but this was because Henson was himself being bullied. Morgan told his mother that, through his own altruism towards Henson, 'the others are kinder to him now.' One Good Friday, he talked to Henson about religion, but reported, 'I was so shocked. He did not know anything about Christ.' Morgan retained an unquestioning, childlike faith until Cambridge.

Kent House generated not just open cruelty but also narrow self-interest. When the school was fitted with hot water, Forster told Lily the 'big boys' took it all. He tried to break through and be accepted, even in boisterous outdoor sports, but was rebuffed. Concerning one snowball fight, he wrote, 'I wanted to go but they did not let me.' There are hints of hypochondria; Forster, we now know, developed a strong constitution. But as a boy he was prone to every passing cold. One remarkable letter, from December 1890, goes further. Forster diagnoses a world-weariness in himself; something which developed into downright pessimism in his adult years: 'I feel so very nervous somehow… Lately I have always been taking the dark side of things… It is very much like despondency… it is not so bad in the day-time as at night, then I cry a lot.' Forster admitted to constant 'forboding' [sic]; he mulled over the following day's activities, anticipating the ways they could go wrong. Most upsetting was – as he found no difficulty confessing to Lily, aged eleven – that he had nobody close: 'The worst of school is that you have nothing and nobody to love; if I only had only somebody,' he wrote – so upset that he lost control of his syntax – 'I shall be much happier.'

At fourteen, Forster proceeded to a still less congenial school, Tonbridge. Immediately beforehand, he spent a spare term at The Grange school as a weekly boarder. He was picked on straight away. Of two boys tormenting him, he told Lily boldly, 'I bore it for a long time and then when they began hitting me and hurting my face, I thought "no more of this" and I slapped their faces.' Forster begged to be taken away: 'Why have you not come?… If you tell about the boys *do do* take me away or I shall be worse off than I am now… Every one is against me…' Lily had other worries. After prevaricating over the lease on beloved Rooksnest, she had been ousted. She chose to live near Morgan's new school. This allowed him to become a day-boy, which had financial advantages and allowed him to return home each evening. But it resulted in ridicule from his peer boarders, who again suspected mollycoddling.

His first impression was to be intimidated by Tonbridge School's size – 'so huge… [that] after I have begun to make friends with a boy I lose him!' Forster never altered his view of the English public school system as brutal. In 1933, he called his schooling 'the unhappiest time of my life'. A classmate remembered him in the 1950s as 'a little cissy. We took it out of him, I can tell you.' Forster's definitive word on the English public school is found in this devastating summary from 'Notes on the

English Character' (1920): its products 'go forth into [the world] with well-developed bodies, fairly developed minds, and undeveloped hearts'. Some evidence suggests that his last stretch at Tonbridge was not so uncongenial. Forster developed a few friendships, and won two prizes: one for a Latin poem on 'Trafalgar'; one for an essay on 'The influence of climate and physical conditions upon national character'. He and Lily would move from Tonbridge to Tunbridge Wells during his first year at university; both are represented by Sawston in his two first novels. But, hankering after the countryside, he disliked both towns. In 1912 Forster would voice his contempt for Tunbridge Wells's narrow and oppressive social values: it was a 'filthy, self-righteous place'.

The Longest Journey drew on Forster's Tonbridge experiences for 'Sawston School', where Rickie teaches. The novel features many of Forster's recollections of adolescence, although, in a gesture of self-liberation, he altered many circumstances. Conspicuously, Rickie's overbearing mother is already dead when the story opens. Rickie's transition in *The Longest Journey* – from being 'cold and friendless and ignorant' at school to his liberation at Cambridge, which 'soothed him and warmed him, and had laughed at him a little, saying that he must not be so tragic yet awhile' – was akin to Forster's own 'going up' to read Classics at King's College, aged eighteen. It was the logical choice; his decision to join the Classics stream at school had meant nineteen hours of Latin and Greek studies per week.

Cambridge, however, liberated him before he even began his studies. A letter survives from when Forster, still at school, visited an ex-Tonbridge boy. His stay had been '*crammed* with every kind of amusement'. He was taken to a dance, and stayed on the floor virtually the whole evening. When he returned for good, in October 1897, he was challenged during his first year, in that he was staying in lodgings, making social life difficult. The opportunities at university threatened to pass him by. But in his second year, Forster was lucky in his college rooms. W7 was a spacious, top-floor suite, with views down onto the Cam and the Backs on one side; onto Queens' gardens on the other.

In his first exams, Forster was awarded an Exhibition, after which he changed subjects for History. Later, he would win college prizes for Latin poetry, as well as the English Essay prize for a work of outstanding criticism. Forster typically fretted to Lily that another student deserved it more. He would finally achieve a second-class degree – more creditable than it might sound today, but evidently a disappointment, given his tutors' initial sense of academic promise. By late in Forster's second year, following the first set of exams in the Tripos, he was told not to expect a first-class degree. His tutor blamed the rote-learning approach to Classics adopted at Tonbridge. He should take up a career in journalism; this appealed, though Forster doubted whether he would excel. He considered the Civil Service, but thought himself neither agile nor intellectually dextrous enough.

Forster continued to study hard, despite the usual protests to all, including Lily, that he was not applying himself. He also played golf, socialised and read widely in contemporary literature. His prize money was spent on books. Forster first bought an edition of Robert Browning's *Poems*, his own tutor's edition of Sophocles, a handbook on Italian painting and a complete set of Jane Austen's novels. In his third year, he selected a handbook to Greek sculpture, and Hallam Tennyson's recent life of his poet father. Later, he read George Bernard Shaw's *Plays: Pleasant and Unpleasant* (1898): 'Wonderfully clever and amusing, but they make me feel bad inside.' Shaw's determination to expose bitter 'home truths' could scarcely please Forster, whose unconditional love of Austen indicated a penchant both for happy endings and for fantastical plot resolutions. His third-year prize money went on John Ruskin's *The Stones of Venice* (which appeared prominently in *Howards End*), a study of the Holy Roman Empire, another on British politics, a history of King's College and five novels by George Meredith. His intellectual reading was supplemented by copies of the satirical magazine *Punch*, sent by his Aunt Laura and shared with the whole staircase.

Forster tried only once to get involved in the 'hearty' pursuit of rowing. Neither coach nor fellow rowers considered him anything but 'beyond human aid'. A reliable college man, however, he followed the crews' progress to cheer them on. Everywhere he went on two wheels, however – like E.F. Benson's delicate Georgie in the *Mapp and Lucia* novels – Forster risked injury: 'To be patriotic I rode with them [the rowers] on my bicycle today, with the result that I cannoned into another bicyclist – or he into me.' He miraculously avoided serious injury. Over his four Cambridge years, Forster kept himself fit with long walks or rides, though he did experience tooth troubles.

Lily came up often, naturally. Occasionally he entertained other relatives. At the start of his third year, he invited Aunt Eliza and his Uncle Frank. Revealing is Forster's soliciting advice of all kinds from his mother: 'Shall I give them a 2/- lunch complete or order things separately, and what? And shall it be hot or cold.' He introduced the couple to college friends, and guided them around the major sights enthusiastically. His closeness to Lily involved plain-speaking, even concerning relatives; Forster was ready to speak plainly of their shortcomings. They 'turned tiresome' in rejecting tea and taking a hansom cab to the train station suddenly to fulfil another engagement elsewhere. Still, he told Lily, 'they are certainly much nicer as guests than as hosts'! Forster's keenness to do the right thing as host reflected his own perpetual delight at being invited, fed or entertained.

He deployed his learning to comical effect in a satire on Aeschylus's *Agamemnon*, published in a college magazine, *Basileona*. The piece's title, 'A Tragic Interior', provides us with an early example of Forster's habit in his fictions of 'tea-tabling' – skipping over the seismic event, to loiter on an apparently trivial, domestic or banal one. He wrote repeatedly for *Basileona*, invariably with a journalistic efficiency of style. More portentously, before leaving university, he began a novel – now known as 'Nottingham Lace' and available since 1980 in *Arctic Summer and other fiction*. The prose is uneven, and Forster came unstuck regarding the plot, abandoning it after about sixty pages. But there are stylish moments which reveal a debt to Austen, as in this bold maxim: 'Events to be truly tragic must take place quickly. However important they are they lose their impressiveness if they take long.'

Forster's Cambridge education was broadened as much by the dynamic character of his tutor, Nathaniel Wedd, as by anything Wedd taught him. A then-unmarried iconoclast in his early thirties, Wedd had horrified conservatives even as an undergraduate, inviting George Bernard Shaw, an outspoken socialist, to address a society meeting. Wedd was also an atheist. When reproached for playing croquet on Sundays, he argued, 'What is the use of believing in a faith so fragile that it can't survive the click of croquet balls?' He was charismatic, too, bringing classes alive by personalising the impact of Classical texts. Forster later admitted, 'It is to him… more than to anyone that I owe such awakening as has befallen me.' Wedd also widened Forster's interests in contemporary writing, recommending, for example, Henrik Ibsen's plays. Ibsen's *Peer Gynt* provided Morgan with an unlikely nom de plume for various magazine articles.

He adopted a somewhat tepid iconoclasm himself. When Earl Kitchener of Kartoum came to receive an honorary degree in 1898, Forster reported the event to Lily so as to seem aloof from it, though he readily followed the procession, ceremony and hullabaloo. The one note of scepticism came in his observation regarding Kitchener's choice of clothes; he 'looked rather a chaw-bacon [yokel] in a grey suit which even I knew was not a proper fit'. Though there were pro-Boerists and sceptics concerning the war in King's, Forster largely toed the expected pro-British line. In March 1900, he wrote to Lily, 'Our great excitement has of course been the relief of Ladysmith,' referring to the Natal town under Boer siege. Still, he harboured doubts about Britain's militaristic confidence: 'What a dreadful war it is; and not certain after all that we are justified in it.'

Forster's History tutor was Oscar Browning. This Fellow of King's had left to teach at Eton, but had been obliged to leave that school following a homosexual scandal. 'I came towards the end of O.B.'s glory,' Forster recalled, 'but he shines out with a magnificence which has been withheld from his admirable detractors.' Browning's impact he compared to 'radium, a mass of equivocal fire'. The tutor affected indifference when students read their essays, covering his face with his handkerchief. He must have been less taken by Forster's timidity and unexceptional looks than by those of other undergraduates. Nevertheless, Browning entertained him with anecdotes concerning the great and the good, challenged him on his preferences in Classical literature and showed him 'six disconsolate hens' which he kept in a back yard. He even invited Forster to play piano duets with him on occasion.

Goldsworthy Lowes Dickinson – 'Goldie'; author of a languid but influential study, *The Greek View of Life* (1896) – was the other History tutor. Forster later befriended Dickinson, revering his intellect and writing an account of him. Still, the two hardly met when he was a student, although they began corresponding soon afterwards. In May 1902, he reassured 'Goldie', then doubting his choice of a Cambridge career, 'It is a very great thing to be a don. I would have given and would give anything to be one.' In his book on Dickinson, Forster selected for praise the 'genius of the place', meaning King's, refracted through and informed by its tutors' temperaments: 'They taught the perky boy that he was not everything, and the limp boy that he might be something.'

In Evelyn Waugh's Oxford novel, *Brideshead Revisited* (1945), Charles Ryder's cousin tells him, 'You'll find you spend half your second year shaking off the undesirable friends you made in your first.' Ryder delighted in making shameless friendships immediately. Forster, at King's, had the recluse's more typical experience of feeling lumbered with the college bores as more exciting figures eluded him: 'One never seems to get to know the nice people,' he wrote Lily, 'though there are plenty of them.' He was hyper-aware of his own neediness, which cannot have helped: 'All this struggling for friends is very unbecoming.' He quoted gratefully back to her, however, a maxim she had taught him in childhood: 'Don't rush into everybody's arms, but be very pleasant to all.' Instead of dynamic friendships, however, Forster characteristically endured endless conversations with one witless peer, since 'no one else will listen to his drivel.'

Forster probably developed a crush on William Mollinson, a boy living on the same staircase whom he later described as 'not very profound'. In February, Forster went to great pains to invite just Mollinson to a 'breakfast party' in his rooms. The latter trumped the invitation by counter-inviting Forster, along with two other undergraduates he didn't care for – and then standing them all up, owing to another engagement. In a letter to Lily concerning the incident, Forster refers to his displeasure most peculiarly: 'I felt very cross, but being "such a lady" behaved in an exemplary manner, being left with the two I didn't want, and without the one I did.' Whether anyone had referred to him as a 'lady' or not, the readiness with which Forster here cast himself as a spurned, female lover is conspicuous.

In his third year, Forster was making better friendships, primarily through the Musical Club. Hugh Owen Meredith, an Irish student for whom Forster definitely did fall romantically, makes his first appearance in letters to Lily around this time. Forster nicknamed him 'Hom'. Meredith was charismatic, manly and intellectually forthright – everything Forster looked for and feared he himself was not. Evidently the friendship between the pair was intense by the summer of 1899; that July, Forster, aged twenty, wrote a long letter to a fellow student, George Barger, opining on Meredith's character, and considering the reasons others found him uncongenial. The facts of Forster's argument are less suggestive than the distinctly turbulent way he reveals his own hand: 'I have much sympathy with the people who do not understand him. If he had not shown some liking for me I should have been as them, and when they accuse him of being conceited… I know not what to reply… This letter is hopelessly contradictious [sic], coloured too much with the question I am always discussing with myself, as to whether I am conventional or not… I'm getting in a hopeless boggle. I don't think analysis can be my strong point.' Forster's self-questioning pre-empted that of his character Maurice, in the novel of that name, who knows his sexual nature is far from 'conventional' and consults a doctor.

In his final year, Forster joined the famous Apostles after Meredith referred him. This men-only discussion group was entering its heyday, and would be frequented by Bertrand Russell, Lytton Strachey, Leonard Woolf, John Maynard Keynes, Rupert Brooke and Desmond McCarthy, among others. Forster described the dynamic intellectual atmosphere of the 'Apostolic Ring' in *The Longest Journey*; he also spoke of Cambridge societies generally thus: 'No one who has once felt their power will ever become a good mixer or a yes-man. Their influence, when it goes wrong, leads to self-consciousness and superciliousness; when it goes right, the mind is sharpened, the judgement [sic] is strengthened, and the heart becomes less selfish.'

Forster inherited a nickname from Lytton Strachey that would stick: 'the taupe'. Held to resemble a mole physically, he also – as Leonard Woolf put it – 'seemed intellectually and emotionally to travel unseen underground', occasionally offering 'some subtle observation or delicate quip which somehow or other he had found in the depths of the earth of his own soul'. Forster experienced a long-deferred sense of belonging, however, in the iconoclastic academic debating. Also, throughout Cambridge, he spent his time almost exclusively among men (which was nothing unusual), just as he had grown up almost exclusively around women. Later, amongst Bloomsbury peers, Forster inclined unconsciously towards its male members, and when, in 1919, Virginia Woolf encountered him in the London Library; she found him 'shrinking sensitively from me, as a woman'. Still, though many Apostles had crushes on each other, some even being acted on, the subject of sex in personal terms, not rhetorical ones, remained taboo. It was, Forster remembered, 'not mentioned in Cambridge in those days'.

Early Travels and Forster the Novelist, 1901–11

Forster was suddenly well-off on leaving Cambridge. Aunt Monie died, leaving him £8,000. The interest he could benefit from immediately, but it was to be used for his education; at twenty-five, he would inherit the capital sum. His book about her would be his way of thanking Monie for 'making my life as a writer possible'. Initially, though, this direction was not self-evident. Forster made approaches to his former tutor Oscar Browning concerning possibly training to become a teacher; Browning was 'amiable but not encouraging'. Aunt Laura wrote to a contact regarding a Civil Service job of some kind, though nothing came of this. She encouraged Forster's interest in the possibility of a post at the Victoria and Albert Museum, although – comically – refused to encourage the British Museum, as 'someone says it is badly ventilated.'

Instead, he determined to travel – not alone, but with his mother, who placed her belongings in storage. The trip had been foreseen, in a sense. At the start of his second Cambridge year, Forster had thanked Lily for her offer to fund a trip to Rome, organised by the university. He told her the trip was too short and that 'I had much rather wait a little longer and go to Venice with you.' They headed straight for Italy on what Forster would afterwards call 'a very timid outing'. Yet it was extensive enough.

They left on 3rd October 1901 and were away a full year. Inevitably, everything went wrong initially. Forster wrote to his friend, future musicologist Edward Dent, of 'a devilish start… comprising wrong tickets, unexpected arrival in Paris, sick headaches, quarrelling, lost luggage'. This led to Lucerne in Switzerland, the traditional stopover before Italy. The pair then stopped twice on Lake Como – at Como itself, and then for ten days at Cadenabbia, where Forster 'got used to doing nothing' in the pleasant climate. He was a dutiful visitor in Milan, seeing all the museums, taking in all of the cathedral, including the roof, where he was delighted by the provision of a public toilet. They visited the must-see Leonardo da Vinci fresco *The Last Supper* at Santa Maria della Grazie, and also Sant'Ambrogio, a church on the site of the basilica built by the city's patron saint. Forster found treating the expected bedbugs with ammonia worked a treat. More vexing in the busy Lombardy capital were the incessant trams, 'which disturb by night and terrify by day'.

They took side trips to Monza and the Certosa at Pavia before travelling on to Florence, passing a couple of nights elsewhere before alighting on the Pensione Simi on the Lungarno, the road tracing the northern riverbank. Forster would use the Simi as the basis for the hostel depicted in *A Room with a View*. Indeed, the novel's title originated in Lily's obsession with – as Forster informed Dent – 'an Arno view and a South aspect'. There was a Cockney proprietress 'who scatters her Hs like morsels' and called Forster 'The Young Gentleman'. The pair spent five weeks in Florence, sticking to the recommended sights. Forster felt that 'the orthodox Baedeker-starred Italy… delights me so much that I can well afford to leave the Italian Italy for another time.' They ventured on to Umbria, visiting Assisi and Perugia. Lily took against the many fellow travellers – English widows, like her, some travelling with daughters; vulgar Americans, and so on. In Perugia the sheer volume of lady travellers was overwhelming. Forster told Dickinson of one old woman awaiting inspiration for a novel; the same hotel accommodated a second who was said to have written her novel, only to have it 'squashed by the landslip at Amalfi'. In

Rome he complained of the 'horrible foreground of enthusiastic ladies' everywhere.

Forster struggled on with the novel manuscript 'Nottingham Lace' for a while longer, describing the unsatisfactory technique adopted thus: 'I've tried to invent realism… instead of copying incidents & characters that I have come across, I have tried to imagine others equally commonplace, being under the impression that this was art, and by mixing two methods have produced nothing.' He felt he was hesitating between the imaginative principle of much prose fiction, and another approach, embracing what Goldie Dickinson had told him was his 'photographic gift' – that is, his talent for capturing real life just as it had happened. In Rome, Forster demonstrated just how impractical he was, first spraining an ankle, and then fracturing his right arm on the steps of St Peter's basilica. Lily quipped, 'It would be just his luck if [the Leaning Tower] fell on him, he is lamentably unfortunate.' In the first weeks, he had mislaid gloves, guidebook, dictionary (repeatedly), money and pen. She found him 'incapable'. Whilst laid up in bed, the injured Forster taught himself to write with his left hand, wondering to Dickinson whether the transposition might not 'result in the revelation of a Mr Hyde' in him. More to the point, he wondered if his many ideas, which 'struggled for expression', might find release.

Throughout the tour, Forster jotted down notes and sketches. But it was first in Naples in May 1902 that he conceived a short story, finishing it in Ravello. 'The Story of a Panic' is a telling work, in which Pan appears to a fourteen-year-old English boy, who resembled Forster; he is described as 'pale, his chest contracted, and his muscles undeveloped'. He is travelling with two aunts, who 'thought him delicate; what he really needed was discipline'. But the encounter with Pan releases the boy, who embraces the waiter at his pensione, and dashes around the Italian countryside pursuing natural pleasures. The mysticality of the Italian south inspired the element of fantasy. When he and Lily saw the miraculous liquefaction of San Gennaro's blood in Naples Cathedral, his mother pronounced it a fraud. Forster reserved judgment. His initial plan – that they continue to Greece – was abandoned after his injury. They substituted Sicily instead, very much part of 'Magna Graecia'. Forster was won over by Syracuse, the town with the most impressive Greek sites.

Some sketches from the tour – 'Sentimental Essays' (1902) – have recently been published in Heath's *The Creator as Critic*. One, 'Via Nomentana', contains a lively account of two Roman lads engaged in platonic horseplay (the quotes at the end are from Plato's *Lysis*). Between the lines, though, Forster's erotic feelings permeate all too evidently, though in an unforced way which often eluded him in fiction:

> They had their arms round one another's necks, as English youths have, and were not mawkish, and when they unlocked and sparred and charged into one another, as Hooligans do, they were not Hooligans. Leaning over the parapet I looked down... to behold that which is not as old as the hills but as old as the ancient world – that which flashed forth in a moment in David and Jonathan but first shone as a beacon in ancient Greece, proclaiming to barbarians that human affection need not be confined to the home circle or extended to the harem, for 'a friend was the best possession of all,' and 'the possessions of friends were common.'

If we bring this piece together with the unlocking of Forster's fictional faculties in Naples, it is unarguable that the root of this sense of release lay in the (to some degree furtive, partial or unconscious) realisation that young men could be sensual, indulgent and even flirtatiously, mutually appreciative in some cultures, however much that remained a forlorn impossibility in England.

In Cortina d'Ampezzo, a small town then in the Austrian Tyrol, the Forsters experienced celebrations for the (delayed) coronation of Edward VII on 9th August 1902. This had been originally scheduled for 26th June, when Morgan and Lily had been in Tuscan San Gimignano, then – as now – heavily visited by tourists and the basis for Forster's 'Monteriano' in *Where Angels Fear to Tread*. In September, they were in Bavaria. Morgan wrote to Dent praising the art collections of Munich, especially paintings by the Swiss symbolist Arnold Böcklin. Rubens, by contrast, he wittily described as 'too prudish', since he always portrayed 'undressed people instead of naked ones'.

Letters to friends such as Dent and Dickinson grew steadily more mischievous. In Nuremberg, Forster quoted Lily in a manner indicating how close her idioms were to those he satirised in *A Room with a View*: 'How I do like a good hotel. You pay very little more in the long run.' Forster poked fun at some German waiters who 'had gold braid on one shoulder, as if they had been hung up on pegs'. He kept up with culture, taking in Mozart's *Die Zauberflöte* while lamenting his ignorance of musical form. Where others understood the idioms used, he was stuck noting character and plot: 'I understood little except the tragic death of the boa constrictor in the first few bars.' Neither he nor Lily spoke German (she had no Italian either). A plan to see Wagner's Ring cycle in Munich fell through, nor would they detour to Paris. They returned to London, taking rooms in the Kingsley Hotel in Bloomsbury.

Italy had worked magic for Forster. An early draft of 'Lucy' – the manuscript later turned into *A Room with a View* – finds one character ecstatic over 'the beautiful country where they say "yes"'. The contrast with Forster's lack of engagement with other cultures on this trip is striking (Germany meant music, simply). Nor would he ever use other European countries in fiction. Of six novels, three were set in England, two in Italy and one in India. Considering his love of travel, indeed Forster could be surprisingly condescending towards places and people he had decided did not appeal. A 1923 letter to Gerald Brenan – then resident in the Sierra Nevada, inspiration for his subsequent

South from Granada (1957) – may have been designed to secure an invitation. It never came, either because Brenan disliked Forster's writing, or because he took against this enquiry from someone he scarcely knew: 'Are not the Spaniards ugly dirty surly superstitious?' National stereotypes were even a natural resource later on. Forster managed to ask India during a 1943 broadcast: 'Don't you agree that the Japanese are odd?' He called Japan 'treacherous and pitiless and insolent... a totalitarian terror' worse than Germany.

Forster may have had a rather deep-seated, longstanding hostility towards the German language, character and literature – though, in historical context, this is unsurprising: it was common. Still, after he and Lily had toured the German-speaking Tyrol, Lily wrote, 'German is hopeless and we do not take to Germans.' Forster took against some US warships in Naples: 'Odious Americans! Why is it not possible to defend one's country without being offensive?' (He would take a more positive view of the United States when he finally visited, after the Second World War.)

On their return, Forster shuttled between Cambridge and London in search of things to do. He heeded the call from his friend, the historian G.M. Trevelyan, to give Latin classes at the Working Men's College in Bloomsbury. Meanwhile, he had written a number of stories, and found Trevelyan's elder brother, aspiring novelist Robert, to be a good reader. In July 1904, he wrote thanking Robert for reading 'The Eternal Moment'. Forster received understandably cautious criticism – but longed for detailed, fundamental critiques, telling Robert, 'I wish you had told me where are the facetiae: they are a most certain fault; and my taste doesn't guide me. Someone told me, many years ago, that I was amusing, and I have never quite recovered from the effects.' (Later, when A.C. Benson wrote in appreciation of *Howards End*, Forster replied that the tone of his comments 'was much too *respectful*; while reading them, I felt as if I had made some serious contribution to thought or literature, but I know that I have not.') A month later, Forster's first published story – 'The Story of a Panic' – appeared in *The Independent Review.* This political journal – whose editorial board included Wedd, Dickinson and G.M. Trevelyan – was a mouthpiece for liberal sentiment. Forster later thought it 'a light rather than a fire, but a light that penetrated the emotions'. He contributed several essays, later collected in *Abinger Harvest*.

Meredith was also teaching at the college. For both, the altruism of the gesture appealed (though they were paid). The college had been founded in 1854, 'to help the working man that we might help ourselves'. The engagement brought Forster closer to men of a different type than he was used to; men whose apparent lack of complexity he found attractive. But it was the (subsequently, anyway) heterosexual Meredith who became 'my first great love'. Precisely what took place between them in 1902 is unknown, but it must have been intense. Forster's horizons were altered forever. Furbank imagined the relationship to be 'very much on the lines of that of Maurice and Clive' in the novel; that is, they probably kissed and hugged but went no further. However, Meredith relocated to teach in Manchester in 1903, where he also got married three years later, though not before having a nervous breakdown. He could not provide the two things Forster longed for: sexual fulfilment, and the companionship of an ideal friend. Returning from a visit north just before Meredith's marriage, Forster wrote of his disappointment at facing being 'cut off' forever – not only from Meredith, but from anybody like him. He dallied with suicide, finding two reasons to resist: 'i. selfish ii. nature ceaselessly beautiful.' Dutifully he kept up relations, but found Meredith's conversation less and less nourishing, and ultimately felt that 'nothing survives but the boredom.' His sharing of *Maurice* with Meredith would effectively end any closeness.

No other employment was forthcoming, so Forster went on the Greek cruise he had missed the previous year, dropping Lily off in Florence with a female friend. Wedd was also on the scholarly excursion. Forster, meanwhile, had read up and dreamt of the many sights; they became underwhelming. At Olympia, though, he conceived another story, 'The Road from Colonus', featuring Mr Lucas, first version of a type he would reuse – the disillusioned English traveller. Back in Florence, he and Lily heard Luisa Tetrazzini sing in Donizetti's *Lucia di Lammermoor*, a scene he recycled brilliantly in *Where Angels Fear to Tread*. On their stay in Cortina d'Ampezzo on the journey back, Forster was frustrated by being surrounded by women, letting slip to a friend that this coincided with a sense of intellectual superiority: 'It is such a depressing thing to look down the table and honestly believe that you are the cleverest person seated at it.' Still, his demands for male companionship were not too precise: 'I do very much long for the presence of some male who is neither decrepit, mountain-mad or clerical.' An intriguing story from Cortina – unpublished until *Arctic Summer and Other Fiction* (1980) – called 'Ralph and Tony', was evidently too autobiographical for Forster to consider publishing, but again plays on the needs of a sensitive young man touring with an overbearing mother.

Spring 1904 saw the Forsters move into a new flat – 11 Drayton Court, Drayton Gardens, Earls Court. It was too poky; within months, Lily would relocate, swapping London for a house an hour westwards, in Weybridge, called 'Harnham'. She was installed by November, and stayed some twenty years, her son invariably joining her when not abroad or in London. He found the small town 'all quite nice', and joined its Literary Society, to which he read several essays. He was lecturing at the Working Men's College and also nationally, for the Cambridge Local Lectures Board on Italian art and architecture. He may or may not have distinguished himself. Feedback from Lowestoft was that Forster deployed 'an even delivery which emphasises nothing'. He was writing prolifically on several manuscripts, each threatening to come unstuck, and taking notes for a proposed edition of Virgil's *Aeneid*.

The first book to be finished though was *Where Angels Fear to Tread*, which Forster completed on his twenty-sixth birthday and immediately sent for publishers' consideration. The evening before, he summarised his personal circumstances in his diary rather mordantly: 'My life is now straightening into something rather sad & dull to be sure.' Feeling adrift, Forster heard of a very different job opportunity. An acquaintance, Sydney Waterlow, had a German aunt, Elizabeth, or the Countess von Arnim, needing a tutor for three daughters, aged fourteen, twelve and eleven, whom she nicknamed April, May and June after their birth months. They lived in a castle in Nassenheide, Pomerania (now in Poland), where Elizabeth cared for nothing more than her huge garden, about which she had written a best-seller, *Elizabeth and Her German Garden* (1898).

Forster took the job initially for three months. He took time off on the journey to take in 'dirty, ugly, mean' Berlin, catching the Ring cycle in Dresden. (A lifelong Wagnerian, Forster would, for a time, give *The Longest Journey*'s Stephen Wonham the absurd name of 'Siegfried'.) He stopped off at Stettin (today Szczecin), where the hot, greasy soup afforded an introduction to middle European cuisine. His diary reveals the depth of his lack of affinity for Germany: 'The country is unthinkably large and contented and patriotic... It's got no charm, like Italy.' When he arrived at Nassenheide in April 1905, nobody greeted him off the train. He was not even at a station. Forster walked through the countryside, struck by 'the most appalling smells of pig & horse & cow'. Herr Steinweg, the German tutor, was awoken, and showed Morgan to his rooms. The next morning, Elizabeth conceded she had confused his arrival date with one of the housemaids'. She made a poor initial impression on Morgan, with her 'indifferent false teeth & a society drawl'. Elizabeth described her children as difficult, and warned Forster he would be ridiculed.

However, he was more resilient than she suspected. The girls were 'charming', and liked him too; on his departure, he was accounted a 'most successful' teacher. The children wrote valedictory verses, though one couldn't make the poem come, so offered gooseberries instead. The workload – an hour of classes daily – was hardly challenging; Forster befriended the German tutor, accompanying him on afternoon walks, during which he tried to pick up the basics of the language. Forster presented a bland, courteous manner, which even succeeded with the Count, whose temper was legendary (nickname: 'The Man of Wrath'). A scientific farmer, he dismissed Forster and the Countess's discussions of book contracts and the like: 'I never talk of my potatoes, though they are ten times as interesting & valuable.'

Elizabeth grew on Morgan – 'She is nicer than her books,' he informed Lily after a week's stay. She got hold of some of Forster's writings in *The Independent Review* and realised her tutor had a literary gift. She implored him to read Jane Austen to her (a shared enthusiasm), and lent him a copy of Samuel Butler's Utopian fantasy *Erewhon* (1872), which became a revered work for Forster, but which led, more importantly, to Butler's novel *The Way of All Flesh* (posthumously published in 1903). Forster admired Butler's subtle prose style: 'The frontal full-dress presentation of an opinion often repels me, but if it be insidiously slipped in sidewise I may receive it, and Butler is a master of the oblique.'

Quite how he thrived in the new friendship later baffled Forster himself: 'It does seem odd that one should be so anxious to please such a person, for she isn't distinguished and she's always ungrateful. Yet one is anxious, and she will have menials, unpaid and paid, to wait upon her until she dies. To want to be loved does pay.' He counted himself among the menials, but enjoyed each of them. 'Really,' he wrote to Lily, 'the charm of the place for me is not its vaunted solitude but the quality of pleasant people.' The location, too, was magnificent – as on one day in June, when the household undertook a twelve-hour country walk. The hills, trees and mountain streams delivered them to a charming country inn, where they ate heartily and played skittles.

Midsummer was too hot, however – 'appalling' – yet Forster was persuaded to take part in a Schiller festival.

In July, his duties done, Forster headed, with Herr Steinweg, to the cooler Baltic climate of Greifswald. Here, a university professor commended Forster's grandfather Charles Forster's orientalist study of the Middle East, *The One Primeval Language* (1854). He was also amused when the university festivities involved a play in which an English traveller, Baedeker guidebook in hand, was attacked and insulted (though all parties ended up friends). The hosts were deeply apologetic, not having anticipated Forster's attendance and begging his forgiveness since 'the dresses are all bought and all rehearsed.' Forster was enchanted by the geniality and generosity of the German students; even better, he found time to tour around Ruegen and the other German Baltic islands nearby. Exchange rates and low living costs made the trip incredibly reasonable. Forster was replicating a journey Elizabeth herself had made (and published an account of). Possibly he recommended Ruegen Island later to Isherwood, who set part of *Goodbye to Berlin* there.

He was back in England for the publication of *Where Angels Fear to Tread* in October 1905. Forster had heard of Blackwoods' acceptance of this fictional study of Anglo-Italian contrasts and conflicts, probably inspired by gossip he had heard in Italy, while in Nassenheide. The publishers insisted on changing the title from his preferred 'Monteriano', which they thought obscure. Getting published was a breakthrough, though Forster thought the terms 'shocking bad'. He received no royalty on the first 300 copies sold, 10% on the next 1000; 15% up to 2,500; then 1/- a copy afterwards. He later tried to reinstate 'Monteriano' for a French edition, writing that *Angels* – which he had chosen against another suggestion, 'From a Sense of Duty' – had been chosen 'hap-hazardly and half-heartedly'.

The initial print run was extended to 1,500, following positive reviews. The best – C.F.G. Masterson's 'A Remarkable Novel' in the *Daily News* – praised the novel's opposition of English utilitarianism and unfettered Italian lifestyles. Forster pitched 'worldly success against complete worldly failure, idleness in the sunlight against a beaver-like industry under grey skies, material comfort contrasted with indifference to life's minor luxuries, life lived for the future contrasted with life living in the past'. Hugh Meredith compared Forster to Turgenev. Robert Trevelyan, however, only 'rather' liked the book, he confided to Leonard Woolf. Forster welcomed strong criticism, thinking he viewed *Angels* 'too complacently'. He told Trevelyan he was not a real artist, but was 'fearfully serious' about writing. The sentimental, he thought, did not come naturally, but he also felt that it should not do so: he wanted it 'reached by no easy beaten track'.

The most striking thing about *Angels* was the peculiar, Hardy-like harnessing of elements of melodrama in an otherwise realist narrative – here, in the theft of a baby and its sudden death. This trait would characterise every Forster novel. Prominent too would be the pusillanimous English hero; the young man who is compelled to act, but would prefer to stand by and watch. There was a continuum between Philip in *Angels* and Rickie in *The Longest Journey*. Forster resumed writing prolifically, trying out a variety of genres. He began a ghost story (called 'The Purple Envelope', and published posthumously in *The Life to Come*), but gave up, describing himself as 'too refined' for a genre Henry James had made his own. He added to Leonard Woolf that he lacked the 'mind of extraordinary frivolity' needed to frighten people. While at Nassenheide, he had Lily forward another story, 'The Helping Hand', which, likewise, remained unpublished until *The Life to Come*. Forster resumed his second novel, *The Longest Journey*, taking it on a trip with Lily to the Loire Valley in autumn 1906. They stopped in Chartres, whose cathedral had a huge impact – 'gothicising' him, as he joked to Dent, so extensively that the dozen Loire chateaux they next visited he reacted against, as symbols of Renaissance self-indulgence: 'Where is colour, mystery and the promise of eternity?'

In 1907 he was asked to tutor a young Indian, Syed Ross Masood, in Latin; friends of Lily had adopted the boy. Forster readily agreed, and Masood moved to Weybridge for instruction. An Indian aristocrat, Syed was strikingly attractive, tall, well built, flamboyant, even kingly in manner. He passed Oxford's entrance exams with Forster's help and presented his tutor with a hookah pipe and gold slippers. By now, though, Forster was in love with the Indian, and recklessly hinted as much, misled by Syed's fulsome displays of essentially platonic feelings. He was invited to visit Paris with Masood in December 1909 – his first experience of the French capital – where they evidently argued over 'sentiment'. In letters, Forster repeatedly referred to his feelings; in his diary, on New Year's Eve 1909, just before turning thirty-one, he wrote, '"Oh love, every time thou goest out of my sight, I die a new death." How can I keep quiet when I read such things? My brain watches me, but it's literary. Let me keep clear from criticism and scheming. Let me think of you and not write. I love you, Syed Masood; love.'

This was the categorical statement, though, which, Forster here implies, he could never make face-to-face. Masood handled the situation with uncharacteristic delicacy, referring to girls he liked, and the pair remained good friends, corresponding across long distances, though often with a sort of tension. In August 1910, Morgan addressed Masood thus: 'Dearest Boy, Are you angry with me for what I couldn't help, or are you up to your old pranks? In either case you're an ass, and I shan't write again until you write to me.' Masood had grown infatuated with a prostitute, asking Forster for advice on how he might make known his intentions. Forster replied loftily that Masood should not hope to improve the woman directly. Women could only be saved from 'debauchery and disease' if men understood that paying for sex was wrong.

Forster later credited Masood with catalysing his love of India, and dedicated *A Passage to India* to him: 'He woke me up out of my suburban and academic life, showed me new horizons and a new civilization, and helped me towards the understanding of a continent.' Forster also saluted 'the greatness of his heart'. What had initially impressed was Masood's confidence in dealing with the superior English; in this respect, he informed the characterisation of Aziz in *A Passage to India*: 'If they patronised him, he let them have it back, very politely, and I have often been amused at the way in which Englishmen and Englishwomen who had begun by giving themselves airs were obliged to drop them, and yield to his masterful personality and his charm.'

16th April 1907 saw the publication of *The Longest Journey*, the novel which, Forster later declared, 'comes nearest to saying what I want to say'. This somewhat personal regard for it would co-exist with a fear 'that it was provincial rather than intimate, and would only interest the limited circle of my friends'. Rickie embodies many of the author's own characteristics, though, inevitably, Forster could not touch on his problematic sexual nature. He gave Rickie a different impediment – a club foot. In the character of Rickie's half-brother Stephen Wonham, Forster styled a pinnacle of dissolute English living. But Wonham was also an example of the ideal friend Rickie secretly craves, and will die for in the novel's melodramatic climax.

The Longest Journey attracted mostly positive reviews, though Forster's first trumpet-bearer Masterson found it 'difficult, elusive, [and] exasperating'. Lytton Strachey thought it a 'dreary fandango'. It is noteworthy that, of all Forster's novels, *The Longest Journey* alone has not invited adaptation into film. It has virtues, but is also replete with Cambridge archaisms, plot improbabilities and, particularly, an impossibly high mortality rate. *The Morning Post* enjoyed calculating that the novel dispatched 44% of its characters. In 1935 Forster admitted concerning *The Longest Journey*, 'I am amazed and exasperated at the way in which I *insisted* on doing things wrong there.' A kind of 'perversity' of method had been at work. Still, he felt the novel had 'never stopped working in my mind'.

Elizabeth concurred, immediately writing in praise of his 'truly beautiful' book.

Forster travelled without ceasing. July 1907 saw him in the Lake District, tracking down favoured haunts of William Wordsworth. That summer he went on a caravan holiday in Kent with Elizabeth and her family – discovering that he rather liked discomfort and enforced gregariousness. In 1908, he was introduced to his first well-established author: Henry James, resident in Rye. Forster feared they might not click ('I hear he likes people to be handsome and well dressed, so I shall fail all round'). James mistook him for the philosopher G.E. Moore unaccountably, and though tea passed off harmlessly, no lasting connection resulted. Forster wrote to Dent of James's 'civility and warmth', but also noted that James had been grand – a 'first class person'; 'I felt all that the ordinary healthy man feels in the presence of a Lord.' Whether from personal animus or sincere literary deliberation, Forster as critic repeatedly assaulted James's reputation. *The Portrait of a Lady* had impressed him at Cambridge, but there was a catch – it was 'very wonderful but there's something wrong with him or me'. By 1905, Forster felt James 'leaves us with a feeling of depression, when he leaves us with any feeling at all'. 1927's *Aspects of the Novel* tackled *The Ambassadors*, which, Forster argued, sacrificed 'all that *really* makes life noble, all that's interesting too, all that's exciting to body and to spirit' in the interests of the novelist's 'damned pattern'. In 1931, he told Cambridge undergraduates that James's 'characters fall into a few types, and are constructed on meagre lines; incident also difficult… He seems to me our only perfect novelist, but alas it isn't a very enthralling type of perfection.' James's 'method was to glance at daily life as little as possible, and shut his ears against a sentence before it ended.' Still, he never stopped reading James, in 1948 belatedly discovering 'the most *exciting* James I have read', *The Princess Casamassima*, whose Balzacian strengths of storytelling Forster wished the Master had developed, instead of his notorious 'late style'.

He again completed his third novel, *A Room with a View*, rapidly, based on the many 'Lucy' drafts he had accumulated. By November 1905, for instance, he was teasing Robert Trevelyan, insisting that he move into his new country house so that Forster could resolve all manner of practical questions concerning the fictional Honeychurch family, which, he had decided, inhabited an identical house. He wrote entire letters to Trevelyan purporting to be from the novel's characters. Like many fiction writers, Forster enjoyed discussing his inventions as if they were real people: 'If you could also provide one of them with something to do and something to die of I should also be grateful.' It is notable that he liked to know of his characters' deaths. *The Longest Journey* had literally borne this out; in 1955, Forster attributed the decision to set aside 'Arctic Summer' to the error of beginning the story without knowing its end: 'The novelist should... always settle when he starts what is going to happen.'

He started attracting approaches from less established authors. In 1908, he responded to one made by Hugh Walpole, five years his junior and also Cambridge-educated. He praised Walpole's first novel, *The Wooden Horse* (1909), though had little positive to say of later books, bestsellers in their day. (In 1949, Forster declined a knighthood, telling acquaintances this was because Walpole had already been so awarded.) Walpole was one of several aspiring authors to take up tutorial duties at Nassenheide. Forster famously encouraged a generation of novelists to innovate in ways he did not dare. But his judgments were never cautious and, when praising, he could cut to the chase of perceived inadequacies. He told Walpole his transparency of style had avoided 'obscurity and affectation' – those Jamesian vices – in *The Wooden Horse*, but that they had also led him to exclude any 'mystery', a recurrent Forsterian virtue.

Once *A Room with a View* was in press, Forster was back in Italy, taking in Emilia-Romagna and the Adriatic coast alone, before joining Victor Woolley, a Cambridge acquaintance who thought Italians 'unreliable', in Venice. He returned for the Florence novel's publication on 14th October 1908. Reviews were largely welcoming, with *The Spectator* pleased to see the absence of Forster's earlier 'freakish and somewhat cynical humour'. Masterson presciently acclaimed *Room*'s engagement with the 'hidden life' of man – 'secret and silent, and often, through a lifetime undisturbed' – comparing George Emerson's sudden kiss of Lucy Honeychurch to the appearance of Pan in Forster's early story 'The Story of a Panic'. Edward Dent complained the novel was hard to read – an objection that baffled Forster without irritating him; he still felt, by contrast, that 'it comes off as far as it goes – which is a damned little way.' Dent was presumably upset that Forster's warning against the indulgences of aestheticism, Cecil Vyse, shared some of Dent's mannerisms.

In July 1909, Forster was invited to dinner by a college friend, Malcolm Darling, by then a civil servant for India. A second guest was a barrister, Ernest Merz. Merz was equable all evening, but hanged himself in his chambers the next morning. Suicides amongst men with a certain secret were common, if not everyday. It seems unlikely that the evening's conversation had touched on anything to precipitate this one. Forster hinted at his own judgment to Darling indirectly; perhaps Merz 'saw something disgusting', he wondered. Darling, meanwhile, became an important correspondent, as well as catalyst for Forster's second trip to India in 1921. When their relationship came under strain during the Great War, Forster wrote in his diary of Darling and his wife Jessica that, 'I never should have been intimate with that pair if they hadn't been so sound about sex.' He began 'inflicting' the occasional story on Malcolm Darling, such as one, 'The Machine Stops', which Darling read out to a Raja back in India. When the Darlings asked Forster to be godfather to their third child in 1910, he prevaricated unduly – first refusing, then accepting, then again refusing. The reason was straightforward though: he was 'one who does not accept the Christian metaphysics, & only part of the Christian ethics'. He had agreed to act as godfather once before, but only to parents 'whose atheism was even more pronounced than my own'. He did write a sort of catechism for the boy, and of course offered his services in his future development: 'If I am lucky, when he grows up he will like me and I may be of use to him.'

Forster cycled to Stonehenge in October 1909 with another Cambridge acquaintance, Hilton Young. They broke in at midnight to eat dinner on the Altar Stone, perhaps having Thomas Hardy's *Tess of the D'Urbervilles* in mind (though Forster only revered Hardy the poet). In April 1910, he was in Italy again for a month with Lily, finishing *Howards End* while away. Not all travel afforded so much pleasure; in June he accompanied his mother to 'horrible' Harrogate, where she had been ordered to spend two weeks taking the waters to cure gout.

There was a sense, Elizabeth Bowen recalled, of Forster's first four novels appearing 'in a sort of glorious rush'. *Howards End*, Forster's fourth novel in five years, duly appeared on 18th October 1910. His breakthrough book, it was trumpeted everywhere and hailed by *The Daily Mail* as 'the season's great novel'. *Punch* rhapsodised over the characterisation of the Wilcox family, 'For the Wilcoxes *are* England; they contain more of the essence of England even than Sunday afternoon, or Lords, or Sir William Bull.' Acclaim was never universal. This time, dissent came from an unusual corner. Forster was accustomed to showing his manuscripts to Lily before sending them for publication. She recoiled against the immoral subplot of *Howard's End* – Helen Schlegel's illegitimate child by Leonard Bast. In fact, the scene in which Bast seduces Helen is not just unconvincing but comically vague: 'She loved him absolutely, perhaps for half an hour.' Forster had no idea how a man might 'take' a woman. In her journal, Katherine Mansfield quipped, 'I can never be perfectly certain whether Helen was got with child by Leonard Bast or by his fatal forgotten umbrella. All things considered, I think it must have been the umbrella.' The novel also affords Forster's complex, fictional response to his lecturing at the Working Men's College. Bast, the working-class man seeking to improve himself, naturally secured much of his author's sympathy. But Forster knew not to idealise. Equally, when Bast begins feeling short-changed by Ruskin's *The Stones of Venice*, Forster allows Bast's criticism to stand unopposed: Ruskin had, for all his genius, 'the voice of one who had never been dirty or hungry, and had not guessed successfully what dirt and hunger are'.

Forster wrote in his *Commonplace Book* in 1958 that *Howards End* was 'approaching a good novel', though, since he did not care for any character, he felt 'pride in the achievement, but cannot love it'. Technically it displayed a number of developments. It reflected Forster's lifelong enthusiasm for music, which would culminate in the collaboration with Benjamin Britten on *Billy Budd*. (Britten would note how the construction of Forster's novels resembled the operas of Mozart or Verdi, in that 'recitatives [the deliberately un-lyrical passages by which the action is advanced] separate arias or ensembles [big, self-contained set pieces of high comedy or great emotional tension].') Forster enjoyed playing the piano himself, if unexceptionally, but still more enjoyed listening to performances. He had used one winningly in *Angels*. Now, an early scene in *Howards End* distinguished between a group of listeners in a highly Proustian manner, as they absorb Beethoven's Fifth Symphony. As Frank Kermode argued, 'For Forster as for Proust, music was the deepest of the arts.'

Aged thirty-one, Forster was suddenly a literary celebrity. Still, even if in frequent attendance at Bloomsbury parties, he was never ubiquitous. Back in the Apostles days, John Maynard Keynes classified Forster as 'the elusive colt of a dark horse'. He was not naturally a joiner of clubs or cliques. About Bloomsbury too, Forster was particularly ambivalent. In 1969, David Garnett placed him 'on the periphery rather than at the heart of this circle'; he was 'more like the Cheshire Cat than a comet' – chiefly because, whenever a party took off, Forster had the habit of catching a train home to Weybridge. Still, like many Bloomsbury peers, he was painted by Roger Fry, another Cambridge friend.

Forster once wrote to Jessica Darling of the portrait, 'I like it, but it finds little favour with the relatives.' Nonetheless, he bought it and gave it to his mother. The austere painting hung in her drawing room, until a passing clergyman looked at it, alarmed, and asked her, 'Your son isn't *queer,* is he?'

Short stories were invariably a hard sell in England, but on account of his high profile, Sidgwick & Jackson eventually agreed to bring out Forster's *The Celestial Omnibus* in 1911. Fry provided the end-papers, an additional selling point. Morgan was frustrated by the difficulty in realising this publication, telling Edward Garnett he thought the tales 'better than my long books'. American editions of *Howards End* and *A Room with a View* also appeared. But 1911 also saw the death of Lily's mother Louisa. Forster had felt very close to his maternal grandmother. Lily's devastation had subjective origins. She felt she had allowed herself to be adopted by Marianne Thornton, rather than succumb to the inevitable poverty, shared amongst her sisters. The mother-and-son relationship became difficult, and, whether it was because he felt her judgment over him, Forster failed to resolve a plot difficulty, abandoning the novel manuscript 'Arctic Summer'. He summarised this peculiar work to Forrest Reid, whilst simultaneously declining to forward it (beginning with an explanation of the title): '[it is named after] the long cold day in which there is time to do things – and its hero [is] one who did not want to do things but to fight. From boyhood he asked for straight issues – to lay down his life for God or King or Woman – and has to learn that in this latter day straight issues are not provided.'

If creatively he was directionless, in personal affairs Forster found few comforts. Syed Masood's letters over the previous two years did (and do) sound romantic: 'Dearest boy if you knew how much I loved you & how I long to be alone with you... Let us get away from the conventional world & let us wander aimlessly if we can... I only wish that you & I could live together for ever...' Masood may have been aping Forster's own statements, or simply embellishing within a literary genre. For whatever reason, he was insincere. Forster subsequently summed his character up aptly as 'sensitive but not responsive'. Erotically and emotionally, Forster was undeniably confused – not least because Hugh Meredith, experiencing difficulties in his marriage, had finally done what Forster had so long imagined, seducing him towards the end of 1910 in Weybridge. He confided to his diary that, when he met Masood the following day, he realised 'it is possible to love 2 people, but not on successive days.'

July 1911 saw him and Masood journey to Tesserete, near Lugano, Switzerland. Masood too had been under pressure from law exams, and Forster was apprehensive beforehand, writing in his diary, 'Shall hope to think over my messy life. Its apparent success is over.' In fact, Forster was surprisingly refreshed by the holiday. Once again he would be wrong-footed by Masood's inscrutability. But a calm came after this trip for a new reason – Forster found solace in the certainty of romantic failure: 'I have seen the worst of him [Masood], but all is well. I bear his going better now, for we shall never be nearer.' In 1960, in his *Commonplace Book*, he judged the trip 'a honeymoon slightly off colour'. By late September 1912, Forster experienced the 'familiar morbidity' he associated with dreary England. A radical change of scenery was required.

India, 1912–13

That October, Forster took off to India, with Robert Trevelyan and Gordon Hannington Luce, another Cambridge acquaintance. He had felt torn at leaving Lily; he knew she would urge him to go, yet mind when he did. At least he also understood it was 'out of the question', as he told Malcolm Darling, that she accompany them. In the event, Lily travelled with Forster as far as Naples, where she stayed with a friend. Goldie Dickinson joined the boat for India at Port Said.

Sport and convivial interaction were not so much provided as enforced among the Anglo-Indian set onboard; the four kept themselves apart, becoming known as 'The Salon'. Forster found the women 'pretty rotten & vile on the native question: their husbands better'. He let slip to one lady that he would be staying with an Indian; she was 'so horrified that after one gasp she changed the conversation'. He had long ridiculed the assumed superiority of white Europeans generally, signing himself in a 1910 letter to Syed, 'from Forster, member of the Ruling Race to Masood, a nigger'. More congenial was a young, blond army officer they befriended, Arthur Searight, who confided his promiscuous homosexuality. He was an avid reader, wrote decadent short stories and was stationed in Peshwar. Forster met him there in November 1912, with Dickinson and Trevelyan; they went through the Khyber Pass together.

At Bombay, Forster went by train to Aligarh to meet Masood as promised. They spent a week there together, but never alone. The next four days they passed in Delhi, staying with an Edinburgh-educated doctor friend of Masood's. Forster's first impressions of India, he wrote to his grandmother's friend Maimie Aylward on 30th October, were 'marvellous... ceaseless excitement and surprise'. He attended a shooting party, but little enough was shot, and – he assured Maimie – 'Of course I didn't even try.' In Delhi and the surroundings, he was struck by how moved Masood was at the many 'relics of Mohammedan greatness' surrounding them. Often he compared the country-side in letters to England, and, on occasion, to the Campagna.

Travelling with Masood allowed him to fall 'straight into Indian life, which is a piece of luck which comes to few English-men'. The Darlings had provided him with a servant from the port on, Baldeo, though Forster hardly depended on the boy. He was not intimidated by the rush of unfamiliar scenes, forms of behaviour and languages he could not understand. Embracing native life meant, among other things, enforced sociability, but he did not mind one bit. In Delhi, Forster wrote, visitors arrived without being announced, sat on his bed and began talking. They then left again without explanation. He was amused by the menagerie. Dogs, a cat and a cockatoo wandered around, eating and excreting at will; they were joined too by 'unbidden guests' – chiefly lizards, though Forster did have bedbugs.

Stratifications between natives and Anglo-Indians were strictly enforced. Forster's initial introduction was to Islamic India, where he would experience the discreet subordination of Hindu subjects. He sought out the Great Mosque in Delhi, finding Friday prayers 'impressive yet ridiculous', as hundreds gathered to squat on the ground. Only later in Dewas would he learn about Hindu customs. Inevitably he encountered more and more foolish Anglo-Indians. Malcolm Darling, Forster knew, was an exception to the bleak tendency; he would inspire the character of the sympathetic Fielding in *A Passage to India*.

Forster was never shy of offering sensual impressions in his letters – the workers, for instance, with their 'beautiful brown skins' exposed to the sun. Food was provided relentlessly, plentifully and banquet-style: 'You seemed to eat anything with everything or all at once.' Elder men struck him as having fine manners; when he and Masood took to their beds after much food in Aligarh, the whole village would watch and discuss their visitors, but 'quietly, so as not to disturb us'. Though Forster had suffered from heatstroke and fatigue in Italy, he acclimatised readily to the constant Indian sunshine. From Agra Morgan told Lily he had never experienced 'such a delicious climate'. Even in the Deccan in the south, where Forster reported it was 100 degrees in the shade, he was comfortable as the climate was dry.

He left Delhi on 2nd November, sent off by a 'Nautch', a traditional festival of singing and dance (Forster thought the music 'excruciating'). He travelled to Lahore, epicentre of English rule – 'a beastly place', he felt. Forster was pleased, though, to stay with the Darlings there, and he enjoyed the Hindu temples, stumbling on a priest 'naked to the waist' singing devotional verse to Krishna. Masood, meanwhile, returned to his legal practice in the somewhat underwhelming city of Bankipore, which Forster later used for 'Chandrapore' in his novel. Forster, Dickinson and Trevelyan met up to find Searight in Peshwar, where they spent wild evenings. It is a measure of the age's innocence that Forster could readily tell his mother how, as a dance grew 'friskier and friskier', Searight insisted on cavorting with him, whilst also jumping on Robert Trevelyan's back. The set even visited an opium den, which, Morgan assured Lily, was nothing exceptional; the natives understood the drug, and in fact the habitual presence of alcohol in India – originally for the Anglo-Indians – posed a bigger social danger.

Forster split off from his Cambridge friends, heading on to Simla, itself 'nothing... but government & scenery', though Forster stumbled into a Muslim wedding which captivated him, and walked out of town, alongside the stunning scenery of the

Himalayas range for an afternoon. The mountains, seventy miles off, seemed adjacent. Next came Agra in November, where he took in the Taj Mahal, 'one of the finest buildings in the world'. It saw his first stay in an Indian hotel. He, Dickinson and Trevelyan continued to Gwalior, a spectacular rock fortress reached by elephant. Forster was at his most amusing describing the approach to Lily: 'Nothing will hurry Elephant, and she is so huge that she has to take a great circuit round each corner.' Next was Chhatarpur. Forster had been invited through the Darlings by the Maharajah Singh Bahadur, a 'fantastic figure, incompetent, *rusé*, exasperating, endearing'. In appearance the Raja was extraordinary – tiny, wizened, lacking a bridge in his nose, usually wearing a dark frock coat , white stockings and socks and heavy diamond earrings. He was also a licentious pederast – as J.R. Ackerley's *Hindoo Holiday* (1932) would document (though Ackerley substituted 'Chokkrapur' for Chhatarpur).

Morgan had no hesitation in describing Chhatarpur as 'paradise'. From the verandah of the guest house they could take in the Hindu temples of the city, surrounded by tiger-harbouring jungle. Best of all 'the nearest Englishman is fifteen miles off.' The Raja met them each afternoon at his stunning, whitewashed palace; the mornings were spent sightseeing with locals, as dictated. Talking to the Maharajah was an oddly formal affair, lasting two to three hours, and taking in his indiscriminate readings in philosophy and religion. Forster found him a 'remarkable' character, who longed for cultured conversation, rather than to rule anywhere. He was unable through custom to invite them to eat, smoke, even enter the palace directly; they met in the courtyard. Still, he treated them to something exceptional for outsiders – a performance by his theatre troupe of a Hindu mystery play. Forster recounted this in fascinated detail to Lily, comparing it to the *Ballets Russes*. (Incidentally, he would see Nijinsky in that company's *L'Apres-midi d'un faune* on his return to London in 1913, framing his impression of the extraordinarily sensual performance of the Russian dancer by way of his own short fiction: 'a humorous and alarming animal, free from the sentimentality of my stories.') Finally, Forster's friends got tired, though, of the isolated kingdom, and, in insisting that his guests not leave on 'unlucky' Monday, the Maharajah confounded Dickinson and Trevelyan. Unlike Forster, they had plans to go on to China. Forster became aware that he had a greater affinity for India than others, including a greater tolerance for 'muddle' and what he admitted was a habitual 'fecklessness'.

Forster was next introduced to the less charismatic but finally more significant figure of the Maharajah of Dewas State Senior. The small, round-faced Tukoji Rao (Puar) III, with his idiosyncratic drooping moustache, was eight years junior to Forster, and had been a close friend of the Darlings since Malcolm had tutored him in 1907. Forster was accompanied by them on this visit. Later Tukoji had difficulties ruling his state, and – Forster felt, because of the sinister interventions of the British – had a miserable demise in exile. Forster told his life story in *The Hill of Devi* (1953), drawing from letters he had written to Lily and others in 1912 and during his later, longer stay. From the off, he and the Raja got on. It was as Malcolm Darling wrote to his sister: 'he loves the Raja and the Raja him.' This part of India was truly bizarre, 'the oddest corner in the world outside *Alice in Wonderland*', Darling felt. A plateau some two thousand feet above sea level accommodated two rulers – the Maharajahs of Dewas State Senior and Dewas State Junior, each with a palace, defended by an army and hosting a court characterised by peculiar protocols.

Forster's first stay was not protracted. From Dewas he took in 'queer' Benares, 'delightful' Allahabad, and – inevitably – the River Ganges, which intrigued him; then on to Bankipore and Gya, departure point for the Barabar Caves, which would – as the 'Marabar Caves' – provide the setting for a key incident in *A Passage to India*. In Benares, Forster consulted the Fakir, who he was relieved to discover did not practise sitting on spikes. They discussed inspiration, as poet and novelist. He abandoned plans for Calcutta, twelve hours south; Trevelyan had already reached it, finding nothing there. Bankipore was 'horrible beyond words', Forster wrote to his mother in January 1913. A single street ran fourteen miles, hedged on one side by rice fields, the other by the Ganges, and lined with shacks of utter poverty. Masood he found thriving in limited circumstances, but noted that his friend could not exercise as he wished; the only tennis facilities, in the English club, were so off-limits. Forster undertook the Barabar excursion alone, though Masood secured a friend to show him the caves and provide refreshments, accommodation and elephants.

Forster passed again through Allahabad at the end of January. He was put up by an Anglo-Indian called Rupert Smith, whom he had met a decade previously on the Greek cruise. Forster was infuriated by Smith's inveterate rudeness to and about Indians; he inspired some of the worst behaviour of the ruling class in *A Passage to India* – a book Smith would read and find contemptible, noting that the Turtons' house, as described, resembled his own previous one in Agra. Forster is said to have asked Smith on one occasion, 'Why are you so much less than you might have been?' He reached Lahore again in mid-February, where the Darlings, he now realised, were practically unique in socialising with Indians at all. By contrast, 'everyone [else] is in such a terror of being out of the ordinary.' Culture did not appeal to the Anglo-Indians; they mostly delighted in meeting each night at the English Club to gossip and drink. Forster admitted that Native States (governed by Indians) were corrupt and inefficient, but argued they were more pleasant to be in, with more relaxed relations between all three parties – the Anglo-Indians, Hindus and Muslims. There was one further leg of travel, taking in 'fraudulent' Jaipur, 'glorious' Jodhpur and Hyderabad. Jodhpur was, he felt, the near-equal of Agra, yet unknown to the average tourist. Hyderabad he aimed for to see an old family friend, May

Wyld, who ran a school there. The meeting was not a success; Wyld heard stories concerning the odd English author's conduct in India. When *A Passage to India* appeared, she – like most Anglo-Indians – thought it provided a grotesquely untrue account of relations between the races.

Forster struggled to catch his boat from Bombay in early April 1913, discovering at the last minute that it departed twelve hours sooner than he had been told. Baldeo earned a big tip in the last-minute dash for the boat. Forster had written to Malcolm Darling in 1910 concerning his resistance to the very idea of the East, which he felt was a legacy of 'Graeco-Roman civilisation'. Darling told him of an exchange with a yogi, who had insisted on the irrelevance of material pursuits. Forster accepted the argument logically. But he also felt that 'in practice one shrinks from this conclusion. The Western world, and in particular the Latin races, have too vivid a sense of surface-values.' Even before he had set foot on the subcontinent, Forster was preparing for India to upset his outlook on life entirely. None of the chaos of India could prevent this from happening. He had fallen for it completely.

During his return voyage, he wrote to Masood, thanking him for his hospitality, and flirting again. He told Masood to share a house with his mother, adding, 'It's an awful pity when people who love each other and might live together don't. I'm coming to live with you in our old age, but till then you must make some other arrangement.' Still, if seeing more of Syed in India had clarified the essential folly of Forster's feelings, he was not ready to concede this fully. In November 1913, he was back in Weybridge, 'teaching English to eleven policemen of extreme beauty', as he told Lytton Strachey. By December, he was writing to Masood again of the 'wretched fits of longing' he experienced. He allowed there were other days when he did not think of Masood at all, and then wrote, 'I expect that's much what you feel about me. In the bottom of my heart I long to see you always.'

England, Alexandria and Beyond, 1913–24

When Forster next accompanied his mother to Harrogate, he left her there, having been invited to stay with the visionary socialist and poet Edward Carpenter, who lived on a smallholding in Millthorpe, just outside Sheffield, with his working-class lover George Merrill. Twenty-seven years senior to Forster, Carpenter had also been educated at Cambridge, but had rejected an academic career, primarily because he could not profess the then-necessary Christian faith. He was deeply interested in Eastern religion and philosophy, read widely and eclectically and had published pamphlets, essays and a considerable amount of verse resembling that of his hero, American Walt Whitman. Best-known among these was *Towards Democracy* (1883), an epic poem cycle on mystical and political themes. His essays on same-sex sexuality, however, most intrigued Forster, particularly *Love's Coming-of-Age* (1896), *Homogenic Love* (1894/1906) and *The Intermediate Sex* (1906). In the last, Carpenter bravely argued not only that sex had, through evolutionary processes, transcended its strict biological functions, but that the latter-day emergence of 'uranism' – male homosexuality – marked the emergence of a distinct 'third sex' in our culture, which would change social mores, behaviour and attitudes.

Forster found Carpenter's personality 'magnetic'. He would never think highly of him in literary terms, but admired Carpenter's grasp of any number of a huge range of ideas, as well as his openness in living with another man. But it was a gesture of the 'uneducated and sentimental' – Forster's 1918 opinion; meant, however, respectfully – Merrill, on his third visit, which stayed with him vividly. Merrill touched Forster's behind, 'gently and just above the buttocks. The sensation,' he recalled in the 'Terminal Note' to *Maurice*, 'was unusual and I still remember it, as I remember the position of a long-vanished tooth. It was as much psychological as physical. It seemed to go straight through the small of my back into my ideas, without involving my thoughts. If it really did this, it would... prove that at that precise moment I had conceived.'

Forster meant that he conceived the idea for his next novel *Maurice*, one whose theme – the viability of gay love – meant that he only circulated it to a small coterie in his lifetime. He wrote it with speed and conviction, happily unblocked, since even in India he had felt unable to write creatively, telling Reid how 'very unhappy' it made him to 'see beauty going by and hav[ing] nothing to catch it in'. *Maurice* was finished by mid-December 1914, though, as he argued to Dickinson, 'it exhibits the emptiness of all literary achievement in rather an acute form,' since Forster knew it could not appear. The manuscript – topped with a handwritten note from the author: 'Publishable – but worth it?' – would be published after his death in 1971. Discretion was innate to him on this topic; the reason was Lily. Joe Ackerley later once taunted him over his secretiveness, citing André Gide's relative openness. 'But Gide hasn't got a mother,' responded Forster.

He was in the first place hesitant over who should receive it; 'I have not written one word of which I am ashamed,' he told Forrest Reid; still, he feared that the book's contents 'might put a severe strain on our friendship'. Edward Carpenter was 'very much pleased' with *Maurice*, but Strachey – whose literary style Forster revered – commented, 'I really think the whole conception of male copulation in the book rather diseased.' Of the relationship between Maurice and Scudder, Strachey felt it 'a very wobbly affair; I should have prophesied a rupture after 6 months'. Forster had portrayed a cross-class relationship not only because of his own desires for working-class men, but also as a tribute to the example of Carpenter and Merrill, whose commitment was long-lasting, even if sexually they were open to other suitors.

Roger Fry thought *Maurice* Forster's finest achievement. Sydney Waterlow, however, would articulate a reservation to Forster that has found echoes since the book's publication: though it may be 'persuasive to all but bigots', it was 'admirable as a sociological tract' more than anything else. Another difficulty would also affect the novel's reception. Forster appeared too invested in the story to allow for anything but a positive outcome – which, in the period context, struck most readers as either improbable or impossible. He knew this, writing to Dickinson of the 'overwhelming' desire to 'grant one's creations a happiness actual life does not supply'. As ever, Forster accommodated all dissent, while retaining a steely confidence that he had, this time, 'created something absolutely new, even to the Greeks'. In terms of subject matter, only Whitman had to some extent foreshadowed him – but even he, Forster felt, had somewhat 'shirked... the statement' (letter to Dent, March 1915).

It is fascinating that Forster chose to send the book to at least one woman. Florence Barger had been a friend since childhood. A socialist activist and sometime school inspector, she was Forster's age precisely, had married a friend of his from King's, and struck him in her maturity as uncommonly open-minded. It was to Barger alone that he revealed the most intimate details of his sexual relationship with Mohammed el-Adl in Alexandria. He thought the manuscript would show Barger 'a new and painful world' otherwise unfamiliar to her. He knew she would not be offended, but feared it might render him 'remote' to her. Subsequent letters to Barger drew on the novel's characters, indicating that it was sent.

Forster's greatest disappointment in respect of *Maurice* came from his decision to send it to Hugh Meredith, the first man he had loved. Forster withdrew his attachment to others reluctantly, and only on recognition of irrefutable evidence of either indifference or untrustworthiness. To Florence Barger, he wrote that, though he felt affectionate towards Meredith, the latter's 'utter indifference' to the novel had made him realise that Meredith felt similarly about Forster himself. Mentally, he cut Meredith down to size: 'to turn a hero into a jolly old boy is a ghastly task, but it must be done.' He would not bother Meredith again, though the situation was complicated by the latter's closeness to the Bargers. He had also accepted Forster's offer of ongoing financial help in bringing up his children (which pledge, naturally, Forster kept). In 1919, Forster informed Forrest Reid vaguely, 'I hear from Meredith sometimes and sometimes of him.' These were times of change. Forster would draw back from Masood in a somewhat similar fashion in December 1915, after he neglected to tell him of the birth of his son: 'You left me to find out about him by chance. I look forward to seeing him some day, but cannot feel that he is in any sense mine, and am greatly hurt.' They were reconciled, but Forster remained conscious that Masood had, for whatever reason, allowed himself to cause Forster 'so much pain'. (In due course, however, Forster befriended Masood's sons when they were being educated in England.)

The Great War had begun in August 1914. Forster first volunteered to help the National Gallery catalogue its paintings as they went into storage. The war he thought inevitable, but it depressed him. Culture and the liberal values he believed in would both be trashed by it: 'whichever side wins, civilisation in Europe will be pipped for the next 30 years.' Above all, he was struck by the pointless loss of young lives. Relations with several friends grew strained as jingoism dominated England and its colonies. The Darlings, particularly, struck Forster as shallowly enthusiastic towards the conflict, of which they would see nothing in India. In August 1915, he replied to Malcolm Darling's enquiry concerning Rupert Brooke's character (Brooke had died of septicaemia that April while preparing to join battle in Greece). He had not known the poet well, but it was 'enough to contradict the legend that the press are weaving around him'. Despite his never having fought, Brooke was becoming – for press and public alike – 'a sort of St Sebastian, haloed by the Dean of St Paul's, and hymned by the Morning Post as the Evangelist of anti-Germanism'. Forster was repelled.

At a party in January 1915, he met D.H. Lawrence, somebody who knew all about crude anti-German sentiment, having married his German wife Frieda just a year previously. The next month, Forster visited the Lawrences, then living in Greatham, near Pulborough, Sussex. He thought Lawrence a great writer, but was more captivated by the man's forceful character, describing him as 'a sand haired passionate Nibelung' to Reid. Lawrence initially seemed honest and generous-natured, telling Forster of his working-class upbringing and its material austerity. The three painted boxes for transporting bees in Lawrence's garden. Forster's reticence concerning his own desires, however, irritated Lawrence, probably striking him as characteristic of the upper middle class. He told Forster bluntly to change his values and conduct immediately. The outburst shocked Forster less in its content than its vehemence. After his departure, Lawrence wrote to a friend, 'I liked him but his life is so ridiculously inane, the man is dying of inanition. He was very angry with me for telling him about himself.' He told Bertrand Russell, 'we were on the verge of a quarrel all the time' since Forster 'sucks his dummy... long after his age'.

A letter from Lawrence to Forster had been supplemented by a scrawled postscript from Frieda. Forster somewhat randomly chose to take exception, replying to both 'Lawrences', 'Until you think it worth while to function separately, I'd better address you as one.' He then divided Lawrence's own character in two; though he liked the 'physically restful' side, Forster wrote, he could not bear the outspoken 'fanatic who has nosed over his own little sexual round until he believes there is no other path for others to take'. They continued corresponding throughout 1915, but Forster had essentially determined to remain aloof. Moreover, Lawrence's subsequent judgment of Forster – that he was displaying 'the contempt of the semi-detached villa for the cottage' in turning against Lawrence – Forster knew to be unfair. As he wrote to Lady Ottoline Morrell, Lawrence's humble background had inspired him more than anything else: 'I've looked up to the class that produced him for many years now.' There was little further contact, though in 1930, on Lawrence's death, Forster sent Frieda his condolences, for which she thanked him by return.

Forster's literary friendship with Belfast author Forrest Reid went better. This was something Forster himself had initiated through a 1912 letter praising Reid's early novel *The Bracknels*: 'Most books give us less than can be got from people, but yours gives us more, for it has a quality that can only be described as "helpful".' Forster appreciated Reid's 'un-Londony' character and lifestyle. Reid, 'a nice and very ugly man', was a boy-lover, prone to repeated, hopeless infatuations with locals, as captured in the fantastical 1905 novella *The Garden God*. In the following years, including from Alexandria, Forster corresponded with Reid enthusiastically. (His contact with other writers when in Egypt was necessarily slight – though he was able to receive and digest recent works of literature if sent, such as James Joyce's 'very remarkable' *A Portrait of the Artist as a Young Man*, forwarded by Robert Trevelyan. Forster also wrote in November 1917 to Norman Douglas, praising his satirical novel set in decadent Capri ('Nepenthe'), *South Wind*, and comparing the island to Alexandria. The poet Siegfried Sassoon, a fan of Forster's fiction, wrote to him in Alexandria, where he thought his unit was to dock in 1917. An amiable exchange of letters resulted, Forster being both impressed by Sassoon's verse and in sympathy with his anti-war sentiments, though they would eventually meet only in England.)

On *Maurice*'s completion, Forster felt particularly adrift. He was too old to be conscripted, but Robert Trevelyan had suggested he join an Ambulance Unit soon to leave for Italy. Forster had reservations of two chief kinds. First, he wrote to Masood, he wondered if he could stomach the raw 'horror' of modern warfare. Second, there was Lily. He did want to help somehow, though, since 'all one can do in this world of maniacs is to pick up the poor tortured broken people and try to mend them.' By August, Lily had persuaded her son against volunteering in this way, though Forster retained some guilt that he was, in heeding her, proving cowardly, or 'leading the life of a little girl'. In a long letter to Florence Barger, he railed against Lily 'always wanting me to be 5 years old again', and failing to understand how vital to him his writing career was. She did not appreciate, he thought, 'the cardinal fact' of his existence. (Of course, if *Howards End* had caused a setback in their relations, now, for the first time, Forster had written a manuscript that he would not share with his mother.)

To escape the pro-war sentiment in England, Lily's intrusiveness and his own inertia, then, Forster committed to a different engagement. He joined a new unit, The Wounded and Missing Bureau of the Red Cross, as 'hospital-searcher'. This involved questioning those receiving medical attention concerning missing comrades. In November 1915 he left for his posting in Alexandria. He remained in Egypt, a country he hardly liked, until January 1919. Though he regularly accrued leave, Forster's anomalous position (since many fellow volunteers were conscientious objectors) meant that, had he returned to England, there was subsequently the likelihood that he might, after all, be conscripted.

He found lodgings in the port city with a retired Greek maid, with whom he established a sort of mother-son relationship utterly unlike Lily's strong hold over him: 'Under her relaxing sway, I gave up wearing my uniform except for my duties, and slid into a life that suited me and into a variety of acquaintances who never coalesced into a set.' Forster's duties involved writing reports on the missing, but also, implicitly, monitoring the health and well-being of hospitalised British soldiers, and encouraging their recovery ('do[ing] the motherly to Tommies', Dickinson called it). A recently published essay, 'Incidents of War', tells how moved Forster could be by stories of camaraderie among soldiers. He quoted from a letter written by soldier at the front, which stated simply, 'All the boys what I mated with is dead.' As ever, Forster did not idealise the troops. He told Bertrand Russell that what he grew to understand of working-class men's lives led him to judge them, rather than be envious: 'I love people and want to understand them and help them more than I did, but this is oddly accompanied by a growth of contempt. *Be* like them? God, no.'

Sometimes his circumstances could briefly resemble paradise. A convalescent hospital was established in the Khedive's country palace outside the city. Here, Forster wrote to Dickinson, 'amongst its tamarisk groves and avenues of flowering oleander, on its reefs and fantastic promontories of rocks and sand, hundreds of young men are at play, fishing, riding donkeys, lying in hammocks, boating, dozing, swimming, listening to bands. They go about bare chested and bare legged.' On the seafront, others spent their time bathing naked. It was a 'happy' vision, designed to make Forster 'sad', for 'they came from the unspeakable, all these young gods, and in a fortnight at the latest will return to it.'

He was sometimes charmed by the then-cosmopolitan city, with its louche, decadent atmosphere and distinct ethnic neighbourhoods, more or less getting along. Forster would write the first travel guide to Alexandria, notwithstanding the fact that its ancient landmarks were long gone. He had further confirmation of the bungling, facetious character of British colonialism, and later unambiguously advocated our withdrawal from Egypt. Still, he found he could not warm to Arabs, to Egyptian society or culture in the least – it was 'colourless and banal', compared to India, he informed Masood. The start of a 1919 essay entitled 'Two Egypts' best summarises the contrast: 'There are a hundred Indias, but only two or three Egypts.' In August 1916, he even compared himself, to Malcolm Darling, to the prejudiced Anglo-Indians: 'I hate the place, or rather its inhabitants… I came inclined to be pleased and quite free from racial prejudices, but in 10 months I've acquired an instinctive dislike to the Arab voice, the Arab figure, the Arab way of looking or walking or pump shitting or eating or laughing or anythinging.' He condemned himself for the attitude, but struggled to overcome it, giving as one example the duplicity of one native policeman. Personal betrayal was always Forster's unforgivable wrong. Here, the young man had taken him to a local hashish den for an evening's fun (Forster told Carpenter he felt 'curiously at ease in that haunt of vice'), only to report the place the next morning when in uniform. Its owner was arrested. Forster characterised the compartmentalisation of the Egyptian's professional and personal lives as a 'particular dishonour'.

Fear of conscription soon meant he did not think of returning home. A first fright occurred as early as July 1916, when, he told Dickinson, the Red Cross 'tried to empty me into the army'. Compelled to undertake medical tests, Forster was, happily, pronounced unfit for service. He would leave behind English mores, too, while away. It was in Alexandria, aged around thirty-eight, that Forster first experienced complete sexual fulfilment. He had anticipated it; telling Carpenter that his 'physical loneliness has gone on for too many months… it's awful to live with an unsatisfied craving, now and then smothering it but never killing it or even wanting to.' The need was sometimes straightforwardly erotic: 'If I could get one solid night it would be some thing.' 15th October 1916 saw a false start. In his own words, to Florence Barger, he 'parted with respectability' that day. This indicated a brief sexual encounter with a soldier on the beach – one that left Forster dissatisfied. It had not been 'squalid', but nor was there any 'glamour' in it. It afforded passing pleasure. Forster admitted to Barger that what he really desired was 'intimacy'; what he felt was 'something more than physical hunger'.

Within months, following an unlucky hospitalisation for jaundice, he would experience an answer to precisely these needs. He met a young, well-educated tram conductor, Mohammed el-Adl, photographs of whom he not only kept; he sent one to Florence Barger. She showed it to Edward Carpenter, who commented, 'But what a pleasure to see a real face after the milk-and-water, mongrelly things one sees here!... Those eyes – I know so well what they mean.' Mohammed was indeed attractive, in a formal, masculine way. Forster particularly noted the 'refinement of the mouth'. In one letter, he regretted the boy's dark features ('unfortunately black'), but only because it rendered them more conspicuous together. Though young, the boy displayed maturity, intellectual ambition and exceptionally courteous manners to Forster – which fact had first brought him to the Englishman's attention, travelling on the tram for which Mohammed was the conductor. Forster had already noticed Mohammed's delicate manoeuvres to avoid treading on passengers' feet. One day in March 1917, the conductor refused Forster's coin, announcing, 'You shall never pay.'

Forster tried to coincide with the boy's shifts in the following months. Finally, they struck up a substantial conversation, when el-Adl asked Forster why the English hated Muslims so much. Forster insisted they did not – rather ironic, this, given the opinions he was formulating about Egypt. However, he cited his friendship with Masood in support. One day, the tram was inspected, and Forster's failure to provide a ticket led to el-Adl, not himself, being disciplined with a fine (though initially the punishment seemed far worse, as Mohammed mistranslated 'fine', rendering it as 'the sack'). Forster felt responsible, but managed through his friendship with the government censor Robin Furness to have Mohammed's fine annulled. The 'crisis', as he termed it, brought them easily together. When Forster asked for a private meeting, Mohammed responded, 'Any time any place any hour.' (Forster recorded the circumstances in a letter addressed to el-Adl after his death, adding further details between 1922 and 1929.)

The affair was undertaken with great care throughout. It always meant much to Forster, not least because el-Adl met an unseemly, premature end from consumption, the illness which had blighted his own family. He never imagined they might remain together in the long term, but insisted to Dickinson that one had to commit fully nonetheless: 'One should act as if things last.' He was aware that, at his age, the whole idea might strike others as comic or unseemly (irrespective of its homosexual character); it was 'the sort of thing that comes to most men... when they are 18 or 20'. Forster called the relationship 'anxious but very beautiful' to Florence Barger; he felt himself 'a grown up man' for the very first time. In July 1917, he forwarded one of Mohammed's letters to illustrate the boy's simple integrity. El-Adl's precise age is not known, but he was perhaps only eighteen.

The Egyptian struck Forster as utterly untypical of his culture: 'there is no Nile mud either in his body or mind.' In fact, he dutifully reassessed his opinions concerning Egypt consequently, but was still most likely to account for his attraction to Mohammed by describing the boy as exceptional. Forster conceded to Barger on 25th August 1917 that he had previously decided that 'natives, especially of the lower city class, are dirty in body and mind, incapable of fineness, and only out for what they can get'; this theory had 'broken down' in consequence of the affair. Still, two months later, an evening of local music confirmed Forster's ongoing suspicion that 'these people [Egyptians] are most uninventive and puerile.' Ultimately, Forster was capable of considerable contradiction on this point, as his feelings for Egypt got confused with those he retained for el-Adl. When preparing, finally, to leave in January 1919, he wrote to Reid, 'I shall miss Egypt... dreadfully.'

Forster initially described the relationship to Barger as 'an understanding rather than an agreement', though he also revealed that enough had happened for him to hope it would deepen; there was 'the physical basis for an agreement'. El-Adl lived in very modest circumstances, owning almost nothing. Forster nicknamed his shack the 'Home of Misery'. (It was, though, a step up from his family home in the town of Mansurah, as Forster would discover.) The vital thing was that Mohammed quickly opened his home, mind and heart to Forster, implicitly demanding trust of the Englishman who, in colonial circumstances, held every advantage, should the relationship sour (this would become a key theme in *A Passage to India*).

Mohammed displayed 'realism and solidity' on one hand; 'romance' on the other, but with nothing sentimental about it. Concerning moral scruples over sex, Forster felt that 'Islam makes less mess' of the matter than Christianity, though paradoxically it was the elder man who urged that they take things further. Inevitably, Forster only ever wrote in code about this to Barger. Between the lines, though, it is highly probable that he longed to be penetrated anally (for which the euphemism 'parting with respectability entirely' may have been used). On 31st July 1917, he reported to Barger that Mohammed had made objections he had found 'trivial' and tried to overcome. By 3rd October, seemingly, Forster had achieved his desires. He wrote to Barger that, 'R[espectability] has been parted with, and in the simplest most inevitable way, just as you hoped. I am so happy – not for the actual pleasure but because the last barrier has fallen.' He experienced a 'sudden placidness'. This surely suggests penetration – the point where there are no further barriers to intimacy; no further distance from being 'respectable'. (Subsequently, though they remained friends, Forster would write with more circumspection to Barger. He wrote to a friend, Jack Sprott, in 1929 of his 'queer' epistolary relationship with Florence; he had revealed everything to her regarding this affair, and she had created 'something sacred and permanent for herself out of this, which fresh confidences would disturb'.)

El-Adl was a civilising influence on Forster. Always prone to shambolic dress, he was taken to task by the Egyptian for wearing an old coat, and socks, boots and a hat with holes in them. Forster reflected on what he could do to improve the boy's position, and discreetly enquired after some sort of government employment as a clerk. This might pay as much as 'five bob', not his present two, and allow Mohammed the leisure time he craved. It would also, when it finally came about, involve his relocating to Cairo, where, as Forster had known all along, 'I shall never see him.' Intriguingly, Forster saw in their transient, effortless union, images of the past, present and future capacity of gay men for romantic relationships. This is palpable in an offhand comment to Barger of 25th August 1917: 'When I am with him, smoking or talking quietly ahead… I see, beyond my own happiness and intimacy, occasional glimpses of the happiness of 1000s of others whose names I shall never hear, and know that there is a great unrecorded history.' The idea doubtless helped Forster justify his own willingness to allow Maurice a happy ending with Alec Scudder. Indeed, on 8th October 1917, Forster wrote to Barger, 'I wish I was writing the latter half of Maurice now. I now know so much more.' The book's 'handling of the Social question' struck him, by February 1918, as 'timourous [sic] half hearted stuff'. But it was the sensual as much as the social that Forster knew he must now revisit in the manuscript. When Siegfried Sassoon gave a positive verdict to *Maurice* in autumn 1920, Forster replied by stressing how worried he remained by this: 'nothing is more obdurate to artistic treatment than the carnal, but it has got to be got in, I'm sure.'

El-Adl moved to Cairo in due course; he and Forster made plans to meet during his next leave period. However, Mohammed fell seriously ill and was hospitalised, apparently with the early symptoms of consumption. Forster, meanwhile, had demonstrated his capacity for jealousy, concluding that the boy had chosen to take his holiday with his family instead. Reading Mohammed's letter, responding to his own unfounded suspicions, upset Forster deeply. Both characters were susceptible to fatalism, and the boy had unhappily concluded, 'I feel as you do. We shall never meet again.' They did meet – though in Mansurah, in July 1918, in the unhelpful context of the deaths of both el-Adl's brother and his father. Forster called their extensive living accommodation 'nearly a slum', but he ate well, and was welcomed by the wider family.

Fundamentally, and without loving Mohammed any less, Forster had taken on board the limitations of their relationship. There was pressure on the boy to marry his deceased brother's widow. Mohammed, himself, was evidently not repelled enough, or brave enough, to spurn the culturally imperative drive towards marriage. He felt the union might be advantageous. As it transpired, he got married, in October 1918, to another girl, Gamila. Forster again visited Mansurah, to find el-Adl still unwell, but recuperating slowly. His wife, Forster felt, was regarded both as 'a comfort and a financial anxiety' by Mohammed, not an equal or intimate. More importantly, he wrote Barger, 'our own basis remains absolutely the same.'

The practicalities of being alone together, however, were more than challenging. Forster grew resigned to returning to England on the war's end. He had the consolation that Mohammed had been nursed back to relative good health by Gamila, and now shared her husband's opinion that she was 'intelligent in her country way'. (He would similarly 'come round' to Bob Buckingham's wife, May.) El-Adl made it clear that he would have preferred 'a companion' – a man, that is – but that social mores prevented this. Forster would see him – the first man to reciprocate his love fully – twice more, on his way to and on his return from India in 1921 and '22. Mohammed, again seriously ill by then, died shortly afterwards.

Forster's friendship with Constantine Cavafy was his other important Egyptian development. A strongly enthusiastic essay on the Greek poet in his *Pharos and Pharillon* (1923) introduced to English readers both Cavafy's verse and the poet's singular personality. Forster recalled him, caught in the street 'standing absolutely motionless at a slight angle to the universe'. Cavafy, who worked for the Department of Irrigation by day, made a habit of receiving company between five and seven each evening, in a modest flat abutting Alexandria's Greek quarter. Forster would go there to struggle with the sense of Cavafy's always cryptic manuscripts, using just his university Ancient Greek. He was attracted to the poet's sympathetic character, including his discreet homosexuality, whilst observing that his profound respect for the Greek's work was ignored.

Cavafy could be a fine conversationalist – 'his talk would sway over the Mediterranean world and over much of the world within' – but as a writer, he was ultimately somewhat conceited; rightly convinced of his own genius, but temperamentally unengaged with others' writings. This even included friends such as Forster, who did so much to promote Cavafy's poetry, its translation and dissemination in the English-speaking world. Exceptionally, Cavafy evidently did read *A Passage to India*, however, recording his 'admiration for that beautiful book' in a letter of 1929.

Once back in England, Forster found dealing with Cavafy's indifference concerning his literary prospects there progressively frustrating. Neither the poet nor the preferred translator George Valassopoulo responded to anything less than stringent hectoring, in terms of sending him a broad range of Cavafy poems for publication in British and American journals, and for a prospective volume of his own. Over a period of years Forster begged that they seize the opportunity to 'give great pleasure to the discriminating' British poetry readership, but nothing seemed to move them – including reports of the unexpectedly large sales of *Pharos and Pharillon*, word of the high esteem in which T.E. Lawrence, T.S. Eliot, and such Greek/Byzantine authorities as the historian Arnold Toynbee held the Greek's first publications in English.

Before his return from Alexandria, Forster was finding all correspondence difficult. He fretted over the deprivation he would experience in England – 'the sense of the luxury here, the misery there', as he wrote to Barger. By 1919, he missed Lily greatly, but suspected that writing to her was making both their worries worse. On his arrival, Forster was indeed more downcast than ever; in summer, an 'abysmal depression' took hold. Forster could not triumph in the war's conclusion as he did not feel that millions of dead had died in a good cause. He felt too that war's ravages had left the worst complacencies of English society undisturbed, describing the 'outward nonsense' of the country to Sassoon as 'still this unbroken front of dress-shirts and golf'. His own class – the intellectual – and its values were 'sliding into the abyss'.

That year, he voted Labour out of solidarity with their ultimate aims, but he disputed their arguments for these. In what would become a familiar peroration, Forster lamented the lack of intellectual ambition in his own country. 'The mind,' he told G.H. Ludolf, a German correspondent who remained in Alexandria, 'is a luxury the next generation won't be able to afford.' He had great investment in principle in the working classes, but foresaw that the Labour Party and unions could, and would, focus only on their material circumstances. Easy or popular entertainments appealed to them, yet – to Forster – 'pleasure' of a non-improving nature 'cloys very soon'. A meeting with striking miners in 1920 was congenial enough, but their pursuit of money alone convinced Forster that 'sentimentally I am on their side, but my intellect argues that clerks, university teachers &ct, are really the oppressed class today.'

He sought to keep occupied. Struggling with the Indian novel he had begun left him 'scream[ing] aloud like a maniac'. Forster was invited to take up 'something secretarial' for the Foreign Office in Koblenz, Germany, but turned this down despite the more-than-healthy salary (£600 per annum plus accommodation) because of a fear of abandoning Lily. He began book reviewing prodigiously for *The Daily News,* also penning essays and reviews for Leonard Woolf's *The Nation*. Following a second offer from the Foreign Office for something in London in March 1920, Forster instead took up the post of literary editor for the left-wing *Daily Herald*, filling in for Siegfried Sassoon. But he remained restless, owing to the impasse he had reached with his fiction. When asked if he would consider returning to India to act as private secretary for the Maharajah of Dewas Senior, Forster scarcely hesitated. He must long have spoken of the country in raptures, since, concerning this visit, Virginia Woolf thought her friend would not only connect with its spiritual resonances; he would succumb to them entirely, and reinvent himself there: 'He will become a mystic, sit by the roadside and forget Europe,' she predicted.

India and *A Passage to India*, 1921–4

Forster set sail on 4th March 1921, managing 'four perfect hours' with Mohammed el-Adl in Port Said en route. It was a vexatious time for all India. The stringent 'Rowlatt Acts', introduced in 1919 by the British, had led to public dissent and, in April, to the massacre at Amritsar. Gandhi, leading Congress, had managed to bring Muslims and Hindus together against the British in a strategy of non-cooperation. In this context, Forster felt that the Maharajah of Dewas Senior was governing his peaceful, largely rural population well, showing 'the security of the Autocrat without the arrogance'.

He made an unlikely choice for private secretary. He did not speak the language and had scarcely run anything. In fact, Forster was more of a confidant. He read to the Maharajah from a range of favoured authors, and from others Forster found less congenial, such as Matthew Arnold, whose 'general dislike to all warmth' he took against. In principle, this occurred daily, though Forster soon found it was more on a monthly footing. The two also played cards. Forster casually oversaw the work being done in the palace and its grounds, but soon realised that his frustration at nothing ever being achieved was not shared by others, the Raja included. (In 1923, he told Malcolm Darling, 'I see no end to the chaos, architectural and otherwise, that informs his state.') With time on his hands, Forster established a Literary Society, but even Dewas nobility struggled to understand English. Attendance was small. Masood came for a few days, but his 'pompous' air won him few friends. Otherwise Forster was surprisingly happy without visitors, knowing that when he left the Maharajah's service, he would travel further in India. In fact, he spent almost two months in Hyderabad with Masood, now employed as Director of Education. Forster managed side trips to places he had long wanted to visit, such as the abandoned Hindu Empire of Vijayanagar. Before his ship left Bombay in January 1922, he was able to take in the cave temples at Elephanta, accompanied by two of the Raja's nephews.

The whole enterprise won Forster freedom from Lily; she had, he wrote to Barger, behaved badly before his departure, being 'not affectionate or considerate'. Still, on occasion, he felt the exclusion of the outsider, writing to his mother, 'Though I am dressed as a Hindu, I shall never become one.' However, he could see no grounds, and had no time, to become self-conscious: he arrived in full native dress for a '*cha-pani*', or 'tea-water' party, held on the evening of his arrival. He was entertained by a troupe of dancers and actors, and was intrigued to find that 'only one of the girls [was] a girl, the others boys.' Actors playing a husband and wife acted out a tableau, in which the wife longed for a eunuch lover. The eunuch duly appeared, making approaches to select members of the audience on the way. A boy pretending to be a girl made a series of onstage gestures indicating sexual congress. Forster was intrigued when the Maharajah – whom, in letters, he referred to as 'H.H.', for His Highness – commented, 'If it had really been a girl… it would have been too much.' Forster recognised he would never understand the intricate mysteries of male-female relations in Hindu India, as he felt he had in Islamic Egypt. The celebratory tone was all.

Three minor scandals attended his stay. One concerned the agent to the governor-general of Central India's ceremonial visit. The usual food was offered to all of the Maharajah's party, excepting Forster, whose Westernness had made the Anglo-Indian visitors conclude that he would decline. The Raja was furious on Forster's account, and made him refuse to speak to his compatriots to register the perceived insult. A second involved Forster's attempted seduction of a young coolie at court. He confessed all to the Maharajah, who simply responded, 'Is not a woman more natural?' Only now understanding Forster's preferences, he fixed his guest up with an attractive barber called Kanaya, whom the Maharajah tipped directly for his amenability. He insisted only that Forster not engage in any passive act, to which shame attended. The arrangement worked out well, though Forster upset Mohammed in Egypt by referring blithely to what his correspondent described as 'foolish deeds'. Forster evidently more readily separated sexual play from emotional commitment than el-Adl.

It was the first regular sexual release Forster had experienced, even if it was somewhat marred by Kanaya's immaturity. The boy tried to capitalise on his popularity, bizarrely coming on to the heterosexual Raja and even proclaiming himself 'Catamite to the Crown'. Forster was infuriated, and found, as the relationship continued, that he experienced a sudden 'desire to inflict pain' within it. For his part, the Maharajah attributed all homosexual feelings to Islam. He decided Forster had acquired these in Egypt. Not offended at all, Forster later described the Raja as 'certainly a genius and possibly a saint' on account of his tolerance (though some scholars have recently conjectured that Forster was duped by the Maharajah, who may have manipulated him, if playfully, throughout his stay in Dewas).

The last incident would be written up in *The Hill of Devi*. A senescent colonel, William Leslie ('Wilson' in Forster's book), was the previous occupant of Forster's position. Leaving Dewas for a temporary but indefinite period, Leslie had planned an extravagant garden in the palace grounds, but had neglected to arrange irrigation. The area soon turned to desert. Leslie was mortified, and, moreover, suspected Forster of plotting against him and having designs on his position. Meanwhile, Forster had inadvertently opened some private letters, addressed to Leslie by a woman. The colonel opened fire in a letter of October 1921: 'I know that some people feel when they get east of Suez that not only the ten commandments are obsolete but also the obligations and etiquette of English society.' The result of this hysterical, misconceived sally, when Forster left the position as expected in November, was that Leslie was informed by the Raja that he would no longer be welcome in Dewas.

Forster retained the impression that all would go better on the subcontinent if the British stopped interfering. He wrote to Lily in December that a tour by the Prince of Wales was causing social discontent, rioting, and even for children to be kept from schools. The 'ill-omened visit' became an 'impertinence', he thought, as 'you can't solve real complicated and ancient troubles by sending out a good-tempered boy' thus. Anglo-Indians were concerned for the Prince's safety, but never considered what he symbolised as he passed through, 'a piece of luggage that must be carried about carefully'. Forster's correspondence to various friends as well as Lily, provided the bulk of *The Hill of Devi*. It also informed his conception of India and especially the arrogance of Anglo-Indian government in *A Passage to India*. Malcolm Darling had witnessed the slaughter at Amritsar; his frank eye-witness account to Forster inspired a darkening of the novel. This all followed Forster's return to England. In India, he felt only 'distaste and despair' on consulting the manuscript. Forster usually could not write up a place whilst inhabiting it.

He left Bombay on 14th January 1922, intending to break his journey in Egypt and spending anything up to a month there, depending on el-Adl's circumstances. He found his ex-lover desperately ill. Gamila was doing her best, but there was a child to look after. Forster spent two days in Mansurah, before heading disconsolately for Alexandria. He knew this was the last opportunity to help Mohammed, however – who he was also upset to find 'irritable and hard' through the impotence of his position. Accordingly, Forster used his resources to escort the whole family to Heluan, a superior Nile health resort, for a five-day break. Forster felt he could handle his grief – 'I shall come quietly through', he wrote to Florence Barger – though when he stayed on in the hotel, he could not stop staring at the empty bed in the room he had shared with Mohammed. A final farewell waited till Cairo, el-Adl softly telling Forster, 'My love, to you there is nothing else to say.'

In England, Forster tried to bury himself in his manuscript. He grew convinced, though, that he was unable to capture India accurately. This was accompanied by a deeper mistrust of what was possible in the novel form. He wrote to Dickinson in May 1922 of the 'tiresomeness and conventionalities of fiction-form… If you can pretend you can get inside one character, why not pretend it about all the characters?' He remained committed to the Indian story. But he also longed to write more immediately in the wake of *Maurice* – more, that is, on a subject his reading public would never care for. Conversely, this meant that the 'problem' he had experienced during *Howards End* might recur – Forster's struggle, that is, to empathise deeply with his characters. His problem – as he saw it when writing to Masood, of all people – lay not in idealising the natives in his mind, but precisely the reverse, since 'I think that most Indians, like most British people, are shits.'

The Woolfs were particularly supportive. Leonard's positive appreciation of what Forster showed him was probably decisive. Forster was never entirely convinced by his most famous and enduring novel. Conspicuously, its author informed Virginia Woolf two years after its acclaim that *A Passage to India* had been 'a failure'. In June 1922, still in the thick of it, Forster confided in another friend that the book's 'fundamental defect' was that 'the characters are not sufficiently interesting for the atmosphere.' Consequently Forster felt he was unduly lingering on 'atmosphere' – the very thing his most enthusiastic advocates revered, but also what, in the form of the property in *Howards End*, he thought he had indulged in at the expense of people, so creating 'a meditation rather than a drama'.

His closeness to Virginia Woolf would slowly abate. Three years later, in 1927, following her publication in the United States of two generally supportive essays on his work, he replied to her infrequent criticisms simply in a letter: *'I don't believe my method's wrong!* The trouble is I can't work it.' Ironically, it was Virginia Woolf above all amongst modernist novelists of the period who implicitly pursued Forster's own instincts, as he had expressed to Dickinson. In *The Waves* (1931), which Forster immediately understood to be her 'classic' work, Woolf would indeed 'get inside' all six of her characters in turn.

Forster never altered his high judgment of the literary talents of both Woolfs, but especially Virginia, which he had first understood on reviewing *The Voyage Out* in 1915. Woolf's 1927 verdict on Forster, too, was not only appreciative but prescient. She revered the idiosyncratic mixture of stylistic elements – 'satire and sympathy; fantasy and fact; poetry and a prim moral sense' – but also noted how precise his novels were in their period context. They were entirely of their time, she argued, and so of benefit to 'the social historian'. Implicitly, there was a natural downside to this. As Woolf phrased it, Forster the novelist was 'extremely susceptible to the influence of time'.

His admiration withstood cumulative personal objections to their behaviour. By 1931, in a remarkably outspoken comment in a letter to Jack Sprott, Forster had decided 'to turn one's backside to them... they will never have the grace to penetrate it, their inquisitiveness never had any spunk, that is why one loathes it so.' He objected to a general tendency amongst Bloomsbury associates to gossip. He once wrote of the circle at large, 'I don't think those people are little, but they belittle all who come into their power.' Still, months later, he was writing Virginia fan mail regarding *The Waves*. In 1934, he even again stayed with the Woolfs, although, over just two days, they scarcely bothered to entertain their guest, spending mornings in seclusion, and dedicating themselves to the sort of creative writing he felt he was no longer capable of.

He struck up an enduring friendship, meanwhile, with the younger J.R. (Joe) Ackerley. Forster had been impressed by a poem which the 26-year-old had published in *The London Mercury*, and wrote telling him so in April 1922. (Forster's fan letters were common, and usually, though not always, well-received. In 1928, having ignored several missives, A.E. Housman reacted against Forster's intuitive appreciation of his homoerotic verse sequence *A Shropshire Lad* (1896), penning 'an absolutely hateful' letter in response.) The two men met in Soho and became firm friends. Forster was doubtless struck by his acquaintance's matinee-idol looks. Later, he advised Ackerley, when experiencing writer's block, to consider becoming secretary for the Maharajah of Chhatarpur. Even before Ackerley accepted the position, however, Forster offered him an overwhelming stream of advice concerning India. He allowed that Ackerley may not dislike the Anglo-Indians as fundamentally as he did himself. Still, 'you will have to hold up H.[is] H.[ighness]'s end against your own countrymen, even if you like them better.' This was useful advice, certainly. Yet, by midlife, Forster resembled his ever-correcting, ever-insistent mother more than he did any man. Leonard Woolf, who always liked Forster temperamentally, once described him as 'a perfect old woman'.

From India, the inveterately promiscuous Ackerley wrote frequently to his new mentor, dishing the sexual dirt on himself as well as the Maharajah. The frequent correspondence during Ackerley's stay in Chhatarpur – alongside letters from the Darlings – gave Forster authentic, up-to-date accounts of the land he was struggling to describe in his novel. He described Ackerley's stories as a 'godsend': 'I copied in passages and it became ripe for publication promptly.' The tribute was sincere, even if it overstates the reality. The friendship led Forster to other sexual *fellow travellers*, including a policeman, Harry Daley, who had first befriended Ackerley following publicity attending the latter's gay-themed play, *The Prisoners of War.*

Daley and Forster became an item for a couple of years in the mid-1920s. Things began well, but they were sexually ill-suited;

Daley liked only heterosexual men. He began to resent Morgan's smothering, feminine behaviour, and constant advice concerning money. Forster meant well, and had plenty of cash for all events. He suspected Daley could not handle his finances maturely. He also objected to Daley's impulsiveness and occasional indiscreetness, but seemed unaware of how inappropriate his fundamentally superior view of himself in the relationship must have felt. Of Daley, he could write to a friend, 'speaking parentally, he is spoilt.'

The relationship had fallen apart before Forster took up with another policeman, who was to mean so much more, Bob Buckingham. The consequences were messy, since Daley had been integrated fully into Forster's Bloomsbury circle, notwithstanding differences in social status and class. A lay intellectual, Daley could hold his own conversationally, and, though they had a long period without meeting – accompanied by some bitterness on Daley's part, which emerged in occasional, unpleasant letters to Forster – he always revered the author's novels, writing late in life that, 'That I am now often considered to be a nice old chap may be due to the influence his main work has had on me.' In 1960, the two met again at an awards ceremony for Ackerley and made their peace. Daley told Forster he was writing his memoirs – published as *This Small Cloud* (1986) – but said Forster had nothing to fear, as he planned to be discreet. Forster countered that, conversely, he had become indiscreet in old age and did not mind what Daley wrote.

Forster celebrated the completion of his novel in late January 1924. Selling it was easy: 'Publishers fall into ecstacies [sic]!' (Forster was unusual in never being represented by a literary agent.) In April he was still tinkering – 'I hope to piddle a little urine over the proofs,' he told Ackerley. Critics were near unanimous in acclaiming *A Passage to India* on its publication on 4th June 1924. Rose Macaulay, like so many, hailed it as Forster's best: 'From most novelists [it] would be an amazing piece of work.' L.P. Hartley thought the 'disturbing, uncomfortable' novel was the year's most significant. Leonard Woolf in *The Nation* applauded Forster's achievement in transcending the 'silliness' of his earlier novel; *A Passage to India* 'marches firmly, triumphantly, even grimly and sadly... through the real life and politics of India.' J.B. Priestley found the novel 'entirely convincing'.

Sales reflected the fact; by the year end, it had sold 13,000 in Britain, and 30,000 in the USA. John Middleton Murry was practically the only peer reviewer to resist offering unmitigated praise for the admittedly 'very fine' novel. His review in *The Adelphi* uncannily predicted the incapacity which meant, effectively, that Forster's fiction-writing career was now over. He wrote, 'The planning of Mr Forster's next novel should carry him well on to the unfamiliar side of the grave.' *Passage*, he felt, had outlined both the ugliness of our world, and also its insignificance. Forster, in a sense, came to an equivalent view, confiding to Siegfried Sassoon that, 'I shall never write another novel after it – my patience with ordinary people has given out.' Typically, he took the good fortune of the book's esteem pessimistically. Forster's diary entry for 31st August reads, 'Too much good luck, and too late. I cannot live up to it.' He batted back some approving comment. When the journalist Edmund Candler, for example, wrote positively, Forster made it clear that, while grateful, he knew their political judgments of the subcontinent – as expressed in their respective books – remained far apart: 'You are in the Club trying to be fair to the poor Indians, and I am with the Indians trying to be fair to the poor Club.' Many Anglo-Indians, naturally, were appalled and angered by his characterisation of their priorities. Forster returned to the question of the 'political influence' of *A Passage to India* in 1962. Though he had not aimed for it, the novel had acquired some, he felt, which he had welcomed, as it 'caused people to think of the link between India and Britain and to doubt if that link was altogether of a healthy nature'.

Forster the Critic, 1924–70

In the winter of 1924–5, Forster was preoccupied with moving home with Lily. His beloved Aunt Laura had left him the lease of the only house his father had ever designed: West Hackhurst, in Abinger Hammer, near Dorking. Laura's demise was far from straightforward. She had first suffered a nervous breakdown, her slow recovery facilitated by 'seven elderly women', as Forster characterised his near family, but leading again into decline.

He installed Lily in the new house with difficulty. She was reluctant, convinced that it would be her last residence. She was 'terrified of death', he concluded. Lily argued strongly to hold on to both Weybridge and Abinger properties, but Forster refused to consider this extravagance. During the move, oddly, a sexual relationship began with a married man in Weybridge called Arthur. They made love in the old Forster home even as it was emptied. More than marriage impeded things, however. Forster wrote in his diary on 24th March 1925, 'Coarseness and tenderness have kissed one another, but imaginative passion, love, doesn't exist with the lower classes.' That left only 'lust and goodwill'.

Mother and son came to love West Hackhurst, despite its traditional character and lack of amenities (such as a bathroom). To Florence Barger, though, Forster gave vent to the frustration to which his closeness to Lily gave rise: as a 45-year-old man, he 'would like to feel what it is to be in my own house, for a minute'. As things stood, though it was legally his, he had to consent to Lily running West Hackhurst in every practical respect. William Plomer caught well how Morgan both belonged there and did not: 'This is his home, but he is only intermittently here; he belongs to the world and the present, to the future too; he is a harbinger of change.'

Forster also rented a flat in London – at first centrally, in two locations in Brunswick Square, and then in Chiswick, more convenient for visiting the Buckinghams. Forster had been using duties in London for some time to secure breathing space from Lily. One exasperated letter to his mother from 1922 implored her to 'try not to interfere... so much'. She was constantly seeking to correct her son, or point out his shortcomings. 'Each thing is so trivial by itself that it is absurd to mention it,' he wrote, 'but they all add up into a loss of independence.' He would find his London space encroached upon, asking Siegfried Sassoon, 'Do you ever have your mother staying with you in your flat? Mine loves being in mine... Every moment some defect is noted, or improvement suggested.' In 1931, he wrote to his French translator Charles Mauron from West Hackhurst, explaining that he had again retreated from his London flat, as Lily had installed herself there. There were other ways of escaping her shadow. Forster sought out invitations from everywhere – visiting Dorchester, for example, to see the Hardys, though the spectacle of Thomas Hardy introducing him to the many pets' graves was a 'dolorous muddle' that hardly raised spirits. In 1924 he absconded to meet an 'odd and alarming' 'little private soldier', stationed just outside Wool. This was T.E. Lawrence, or Lawrence of Arabia.

Forster confronted what became, astonishingly, a forty-five-year fictional silence directly in public, reiterating variations of the phrase, 'I somehow dried up', by way of explanation. In private, he conceded that the seedbed of his novels – romantic dalliance; misunderstandings between the sexes; the drive of plots towards heterosexual union and/or marriage – confounded him. He would write a number of gay-themed stories. Some were semi-pornographic, largely for his own amusement (though those he had written before *Passage* he symbolically consigned to flames in 1922, in a superstitious gesture – Forster called it 'sacrificial' – to bring that novel to completion). Many of the better ones were collected posthumously in *The Life to Come*. Of the title story, which he shared with Sassoon in 1923, Forster wrote, 'Why can't I always be writing things like this – it is the only freedom. I shouldn't want friends or bodily gratifications then.' He also revised *Maurice* substantially, adding the final chapter, following Christopher Isherwood's encouraging reading of the manuscript in 1933. Maurice, Isherwood felt, was 'one of the few truly noble characters of fiction'. Forster's *Commonplace Book* reveals that he occasionally entertained writing another novel. Nothing came of it.

Believing that it was 'better to dribble than to dry up' – Frank Kermode's phrase – Forster progressively devoted himself to criticism. He 'became a sage', in Jack Sprott's words. This didn't impress everybody. D.H. Lawrence thought him 'rather a piffle' as a critic. It was curious, too, in that few authors had less time for criticism than Forster. When a letter arrived in 1930 praising his *Aspects of the Novel*, Forster rebuked the sender, telling her 'not [to] pay much attention either to it or to any other work of literary criticism'. In 1938, Rose Macaulay would begin the steady stream of books devoted to his books with *The Writings of E.M. Forster*; he thought the study 'considerate and tactful, gratifying and... intelligent, but tamely conceived and badly written'.

Forster's pantheon as critic was select and consistent. (He was, as Furbank put it, 'the great simplifier'.) Three authors had helped most in his own discovery of literary style: Austen, Butler and Proust. This was different to addressing the matter of literary 'greatness' at large. The greats, he thought, were Dante, Gibbon and Tolstoy. Of Gibbon's *Autobiography*, he wrote in 1910, 'There are passages in it that are more than "correct", and on the border line of beauty. What a giant he is – greatest historian & greatest name of the 18th century *I* say.' He also had a negative canon, in one broadcast censuring Augustine's *Confessions*, Machiavelli's *The Prince*, Swift's *Gulliver's Travels* and anything by Carlyle.

We should not think of these citations as advocacy. In this respect, Forster could be somewhat snobbish. In a 1937 lecture to undergraduates, he spoke at length of Proust's essential curiosity, then added, 'Many of you will have read Proust, but those who haven't – I am not going to recommend him. He will not help you in what I suppose to be your problems, he will take up too much of your time, and you have not much time. He represents an age which has just closed, an age of private lives, and I think that's even more remote from you than is the prewar age.' Conversely, his literary round-ups for the radio in India were sometimes packed with the most bizarre recommendations, such as a biography of the deeply corrupt, delusional decadent novelist Frederick Rolfe. Just what the educated, thirty-year-old Indian man – Forster's imaginary listener – would have made of this must be imagined. Sometimes he acknowledged the weirdness of the whole exercise, telling Indian listeners in 1947 apropos Stefan Zweig, 'I don't expect Europe means very much to you.' Through the war, however, his broadcasts to the East took on a didactic character which Forster was surprisingly comfortable with, since 'Literature and Democracy are natural allies.' He believed the Second World War 'partly a battle of books against bonfires'. In 1943, recommending some staples of the German canon, he added that Nazis 'ban German culture. We don't.'

He almost accidentally became one of the BBC Third Programme's most recognised voices of cultural authority. Forster could be ambivalent about the programmes' value, telling Isherwood in 1932 – the year he started – that broadcasting was 'worse than schoolmastering, it might be argued'. Yet he prepared for each session assiduously, worrying away at the inevitable inscrutability of the listener, and at the appropriate intellectual level. He also allowed the transcripts of a good number of pieces to be included in 1951's *Two Cheers for*

Democracy. Forster could happily accept the ephemeral, trivial nature of his book recommendations in a world he understood less and less, one in whose context the role of literature was no longer clear. He felt, bluntly, that all fiction, and possibly all literature, faced a death sentence. In 1937, Forster argued on air that 'no serious person [today] has the time to be a great writer… I wonder indeed whether there will be any more literature.' Forster next began recording monthly for the Corporation's Eastern radio service – known, cryptically, as 'The Purple Network', and broadcast to India (a colony until 1947) as well as the Far East. His first producer here was George Orwell, who was succeeded by John Arlott. Orwell wisely told Arlott, 'Forster is no work at all; but don't try to alter him.' For both services, Forster scripted a regular round-up of literary news (obituaries chiefly), reviews of recent publications and occasional puffs for old classics he felt relevant to the times.

At the same time, he continued to encourage the many younger authors seeking him out. One, naturally, was T.E. Lawrence, who solicited Forster's help with finessing *Seven Pillars of Wisdom*, which the latter was convinced was '*a very great work*'. With jokey modesty, Forster noted his appropriateness: 'Have written some novels, also done journalism and historical essays; no experience of active life, no power of managing men, no Oriental languages, but some knowledge of Orientals.' Lawrence made sure that Forster received one of the handsome 'Subscriber's Text' editions of 1926. Forster dedicated his 1928 story collection *The Eternal Moment* to Lawrence 'in the absence of anything else'. The 'else' may have referred to the gay stories, which he sent to the intrigued soldier privately, though Lawrence only laughed at 'The Life to Come', informing Forster – to whom he had evidently confided the detail of his (supposed) rape at the hands of Turks, 'We're different, aren't we. I make an awful fuss about what happened to me: & you invent a voluntary parallel [to it], about which the two victims make no bones at all.' Forster disputed this reading of his tale, but forgave him, sending on 'Dr Woolacott', which Lawrence gratifyingly considered 'the most powerful thing I have ever read'. There was the sparring of mutual acclaim – 'I believe that you are a "greater genius than myself"' (E.M.F. to T.E.L.); 'I'm not of the class fit to read your writing' (T.E.L. to E.M.F.) – and occasional visits to Lawrence at Clouds Hill in Dorset. One was planned when Lawrence's death in a motorcycling accident intervened. On 3rd October 1936, Forster attended the unveiling of a 'hatchet-faced' plaque of Lawrence at Oxford High School, which he had attended. The event was chiefly notable to Forster for a speech given by Winston Churchill, the one politician he despised. But for concerns regarding a prospective suit for libel, Forster was to have edited a posthumous collection of Lawrence's correspondence. Another writer he befriended and admired greatly was the South African William Plomer, introduced by the Woolfs in 1929, when Plomer was twenty-five. He wrote a memorable description of Forster's physical impression as 'the reverse of a dandy'; passers-by might think him 'a dim provincial of settled habits and take no more notice of him'. On literary matters the two were mutually respectful, Forster thinking highly of Plomer's second novel *Sado* (1931). Plomer was Forster's initial choice of biographer, prior to P.N. Furbank.

In 1927, Forster delivered the Clark Lectures in Cambridge on the subject of fiction. These were deliberately 'ramshackly' constructs (his term), though they were well received when published as *Aspects of the Novel*. He consistently defended the freedom of novelists, too, finding himself prepared to act as witness on Radclyffe Hall's behalf in 1928, in the case concerning her lesbian-themed *The Well of Loneliness*, charged under the 1857 Obscene Publications Act. Fortunately, Forster and other witnesses were not called, or he may have had to finesse his true view of the novel's insignificance as literature. Questions of censorship had long interested him. In 1907 Forster had corresponded with Edward Garnett over the latter's play *The Breaking Point*, which was denied a performance licence by the Lord Chamberlain but then published as *A Censored Play*. In 1960, he would defend Lawrence's *Lady Chatterley's Lover* against the charge of obscenity – doubly ironic, this, given his view of that book as inferior and the way his friendship with Lawrence had ended.

Many works threatened with various forms of legal prosecution and suppression were suspected because of sexual frankness, particularly in respect of homosexuality. One such was James Hanley's 1931 sea saga, *Boy*, which Forster unusually did not agree to support publicly, but did admire. It was banned. Forster kept to his decision that he would not divulge his sexual character whilst Lily lived. He gently disappointed Ackerley in thus refusing to write a foreword to *Hindoo Holiday* (1932). In 1942, he helped Ackerley draft a letter concerning a Welsh police witch-hunt that resulted in several attempted suicides and one successful one. He did not sign it. In October 1953, Forster wrote a breakthrough article, 'Society and the Homosexual' for the *New Statesman and Nation*. The reason was straightforward; Lily had died, aged ninety, in 1945. Forster urged the case for the repeal of laws against male-male sexual acts. Yet again, the piece was far from a proclamation of rights, and far from open. He quoted a judge, arguing for some 'humane method for dealing with homosexual cases', himself concluding, with a rather pathetic resort to irony, 'in such indications... there is certainly ground for hope.' In the 1960s, some friends, including Ackerley, urged Forster to publish the gay stories he had circulated. But Forster was mindful that the law against homosexual acts still stood (until 1967). He told Ackerley, 'I'm afraid I'm a coward.' Paradoxically, though his mother was the initial concern, well before her death in 1945 Forster had a different cause to continue his silence, given how frequently his name and Bob Buckingham's were linked ('Everyone connects him with me,' he told Isherwood in 1938) and the scandal this might cause the policeman and his family.

Forster kept busy. In 1926 he attended a physiological congress in Stockholm, detouring on his return, taking in Copenhagen and Elsinore, the 'Hamlet castle', which he saw with a young newspaper seller he picked up called Aage, whom he lied to, and was lied back to in return. In 1929, he accompanied George and Florence Barger on a long trip to South Africa, which did not appeal. A tour of the diamond mines left Forster convinced it was 'the most imbecile industry in the world'. The Rand Club in Johannesburg he characterised to Lily as a 'notorious haunt of millionaires and swindlers'. 'Most Africans', he concluded to Ackerley, meaning blacks, seemed 'simply heart-broken… trade and Christianity together have done them in.' The excursion gave him another chance to see Cavafy at home in Alexandria. He rejoiced in Egypt's liberation from colonial rule, telling Ackerley, 'Egypt after the British Empire is more wonderful, beautiful and amusing than can well be imagined.'

He was active in the international writers' organisation PEN, attending a number of international conferences. He twice acted as president of the National Council for Civil Liberties, in 1934 and 1942. In 1934 his generous (and self-censored) account of Goldsworthy Lowes Dickinson appeared. That same year his stewardship of the NCCL involved him in considerable efforts to prevent the passing into law of an Incitement to Disaffection (or 'Sedition') Bill). It was passed, but much weakened, bringing Forster and the organisation credit. June 1935 found him in Paris, attending an 'International Congress of Writers'. This turned out to be a somewhat self-appointed claque of lesser Communist sympathisers. Forster fought in vain to have the forum expand, with the support of fellow liberal Aldous Huxley, but nothing came of this. In Paris he summarised his own liberalism as a sort of dissent from Communism: 'I am not a Communist, though perhaps I might be one if I was a younger and a braver man, for in Communism I can see hope. It does many things which I think evil, but I know that it intends good.' *Abinger Harvest* (1936), an essay collection, involved him in libel proceedings. One essay, dating from 1919, concerned a farcical dispute between two British engineers as to how to treat the waters of the Nile. Forster's essay drew heavily on one side of the debate; allowing republication, he was unaware that the second party had won a libel action against the first, for the very article which had formed the basis of Forster's own piece, 'A Flood in the Office'. Forster had to pay damages and costs. The offending article was removed. He was simultaneously suffering after a serious, two-stage operation on his prostate (December 1935 – February 1936).

His circle of friends continued to widen; Forster met Christopher Isherwood in 1932. They were already fans of one another's work, and their shared homosexuality gave them much to discuss – not least the manuscript of *Maurice*, which Isherwood wrote in huge support of in 1933, a gesture which inspired Forster to return to the work. Isherwood was, like Ackerley, keen on sexual openness, and encouraged Forster to think that the novel might be published one day. Forster, however, suspected he was living in a rarified, metropolitan bubble of liberalism and supportiveness: 'The more one meets decent & sensible people, of whom there are now a good few, the more does one forget the millions of beasts and idiots who still prowl in the darkness, ready to gibber and devour.' Perversely, he almost longed for the self-oppression which had characterised his twenties, when he shamefully hid 'a fatal secret' about which everything was clear. By 1948, he could tell Isherwood that he was 'ashamed at shirking publication' of *Maurice*, but felt 'formidable' obstacles remained. Likewise he prevaricated over Isherwood's invitations to host him in Berlin. In 1939 Forster still planned to go, but felt unable to presently since his mother 'thinks Hitler will cut my hand off'. It was, of course, a joke – but partly at his own expense. He was sixty.

Forster belittled his own concerns readily – 'tea-tabling' his own life, in fact; that is, loitering on the incidental moment, rather than the seismic. (The term was invented by Isherwood's friend, author Edward Upward, and was therefore written up by Upward's alter ego Chalmers in Isherwood's fictional memoir *Lions and Shadows* (1938). The Isherwood-Upward tribute to their master was sincere and unconditional; Chalmers argued in the book that, 'Forster's the only one who understands what the modern novel ought to be.')

Sometimes this humility involved little more than the national Stiff Upper Lip. Forster broadcast in 1939 that 'Herr Hitler has chosen to make himself a nuisance,' as if Third Reich expansionism were a matter of schoolboy pranks. On hearing tales of sexual derring-do in Berlin, he wrote to Isherwood, 'My life is a water-colour rendering of yours: a burst water-pipe instead of a frozen radiator, cough and cold instead of clap, failure to start an article... instead of a novel, and a £50 loan to Mrs. Morgan at the garage instead of an American debt.' (The sexual free-for-all wouldn't have offended Forster; he told Furbank in 1953, 'Orgies are so important, and they are things one knows *nothing* about.') Forster couldn't do Grand Guignol. In 1944, he was underplaying the rocket bombardment of the capital, telling Isherwood calmly that 'we are not at the moment at our mental best in the London area.'

The horrors of Nazism threw up difficulties both complex and ominous long before the outbreak of war itself – which Forster, like everyone in England barring Chamberlain and a few cranks, had long grown resigned to. Isherwood was in Portugal with his German lover Heinz by 1936, awaiting the boy's summons back to the Fatherland (and, naturally, conscription): 'The postman is awaited daily like an executioner.' Notoriously, he and Auden would leave Europe for the States in 1939. Forster stayed, doing much in the press and elsewhere to criticise the vocal censure of his two friends. This censure was certainly informed by jingoism, homophobia and philistinism; it was the same 'prim ungenerosity' Forster remembered from the previous war, he told Richard, Isherwood's brother. Still, it remains easy to see how Orwell's contempt for the pair better caught the mood of a country braced for the fight of its life than Forster's careful, even pedantic insistence that valuing freedoms meant allowing people like Auden and Isherwood to make choices that might offend you.

If popular opinion interpreted their departure as jumping from a sinking ship to save their skins, some part of Forster even understood the judgment. In an early letter to Isherwood in America, he noted pithily that 'it is clearly your job to see us sink from a distance, if sink we do.' Forster intimated that he might have joined them if urged to, 'but was not sure it suited you and Wystan, and have been too afraid to come since' (17th June 1939). It seems that, deep down, a part of Forster at least did resent the flight to America. Already in 1939, Forster admitted, 'I don't seem to want to write letters to you,' and found Isherwood's American novels unsympathetic.

It seems obvious that worries concerning Lily would not have allowed Forster to leave. But there was somebody else whom he now also had to consider. Throughout the 1930s, Forster's life was lifted, and at times complicated, by a developing relationship with the second policeman of his life, Bob Buckingham. He met the dusky, dashing, basically heterosexual keen sportsman and rower in 1931. Buckingham must have seemed the answer to Forster's erotic needs, which he would later express in vivid terms in the unpublished essay he repeatedly returned to entitled 'Sex': 'I want to love a strong young man of the lower classes and be loved by him and even hurt by him.' He went on to identify this masochistic aspect to his character with some very extreme sexual desires, such as coprophilia, which he nevertheless was not attracted to.

Forster's sexual nature, combined with the suppressed hostility at the crowd of women who had brought him up and attended his every childhood move, led him readily into misogyny. He noted in 'Sex' that 'I have never tried to turn a man into a girl, as Proust did with Albertine, for this seemed derogatory to me as a writer.' The sense is that the character, or model for the character, would be the one being demeaned. It was a fascinating comment, coming from one who, to many, wrote so well about women's perceptions and needs, but who also described the suffragette Christabel Pankhurst as 'very able, very clever and very unpleasant'. He admitted privately to having spoken 'with false enthusiasm of women's rights': 'She [Woman] shall have all she wants. I can still get away from her. I grudged her nothing except my company.'

The degree of Forster's masochism cannot be fully known. Two poems reproduced in *The Creator as Critic*, however, offer clues, as well as some suggestions as to the likely content of the stories Forster burnt in 1922. Forster's own view was that he was 'not a poet', and these attempts were evidently written to arouse the author sexually – a little like W.H. Auden's infamous 'The Platonic Blow', unpublished in the poet's lifetime. 'A Soldier of the Devil's Own' and 'Vulcan and Adonis' are dated 1961, but may well have been written much earlier and merely copied out later. In the first, a soldier sets about corrupting a ploughboy, but ends up literally skewered for his pains. The second finds both young figures of legend masturbating in a forest, separately; they then couple, reaching 'realms beyond the powers of speech':

They wrestle demigod and god,
Till Vulcan lubricates his rod
Jumps on Adonis from behind
And puts it through his tender rind.

Adonis is anally raped by Vulcan, and predictably learns to enjoy it:

He bursts, he lets himself be burst,
Accepts young Vulcan's liquid fires
And not unrecompensed expires.

These verses will not affect Forster's literary reputation either way, as 'The Platonic Blow' has not for Auden. They are suggestive evidence, though, of how intrinsically he connected sexual pleasure to the enactment of strong power dialectics. It may be facetious to note that Forster conceded when broadcasting on

Samuel Butler that he himself had 'the sort of mind which likes to be taken unawares'. Whatever the precise nature of his sexual needs, though, it is clear that it was in sex alone that he sought humiliation, if anywhere, and not outside it. In social and intellectual terms, Forster liked to dominate his sexual partners.

From 1932, Buckingham was happily married – to a nurse, May. Forster was unperturbed from the outset, having understood all along that their initial closeness had only ever resulted because Buckingham was disappointed after the breaking-off of an earlier engagement. Moreover, 'I'm quite sure,' he told Jack Sprott, 'that his feeling for me is something he has never had before. It's a spiritual feeling which has spread to my physique... so that my lack of youth and presence... are here no disadvantage.' He would call in constantly in Chiswick, later inviting both Buckinghams to holiday with him. He offered advice and money for the education of their son, Robert. When the latter died in his late twenties, already married with two sons, both bearing the middle name of Morgan, Forster set up monthly payments to secure the family home. Forster was, like Proust, almost universally generous – both to such friends (he funded an operation for Harry Daley's mother), and to those heterosexual men with whom he had had brief relationships. One such, Frank Vicary, a miner turned pig-breeder, was so grateful for this charity he also named one boy Morgan. Buckingham though has the undoubted claim to becoming the love of Forster's (later) life. When, for example, Forster brought Mohammed el-Adl to mind in 1963, he was very clear in telling William Plomer, 'With one exception – and that a tremendous one – he has been the greatest thing in my life.' Forster, May and Buckingham entered into a sort of understanding which endured until his death. After the war, the Buckinghams relocated to Coventry, where Bob became a probationary officer, Forster was a frequent guest.

The chief problem, inevitably, was the necessarily incidental nature of their meetings. Forster wanted more. He would mostly reverse his initial, jealous judgment of May – as 'domineering sly and *knowing*' (to Jack Sprott in 1932) – though the underlying note of misogyny resurfaces in a reference to Buckingham of May's 'feminine technique' in 1940. The deeper problem was Forster's sexual and emotional neediness: 'When I cannot "get what I want" I have tempers... they are canny & calculating & non-suicidal and I hate them.' There would be characteristically pointed comments in letters to Buckingham along similar lines: 'If you call living a full life seeing me once a fortnight, I don't' (19th July 1939); 'You never come and stop with me in the flat these days... week after week is never the right week' (28th February 1940). When May told Forster that Buckingham had been having an affair behind her back during the Second World War, he replied archly, 'I console, and next have breakdown of grief myself.' Even at the age of eighty-seven, Forster could register his 'hurt' to Buckingham from Cambridge at plans to visit the Boat Race without him: 'We have seen it together, when we could, since 1930.' Latterly, Buckingham would claim that the relationship had never been sexual, and that he had been astonished to discover that Forster was gay. But the evidence doesn't stack up. Forster wrote assuring Buckingham he had no sexually transmitted diseases; he wrote to Ackerley – after he and Buckingham had spent two years 'violently in liking' – that he had consulted a doctor about the sexual aspect, and had been told 'that this sort of thing isn't natural and that nature takes it out of you somehow if you go against her.' The most critical thing, though, was that Forster found emotional succour. A 1932 entry in his *Commonplace Book* records, 'I have been happy for two years... I want to write it down before it gets spoiled by pain.'

He continued to review regularly, if – as was the custom – anonymously, in the books pages of *The Listener*, for which Ackerley had been appointed literary editor in 1935; they worked together for a quarter of a century. Forster based himself in West Hackhurst, but was regularly in London, also taking holidays in Dover, with friends such as Plomer. He preferred the freedom afforded by renting a flat over staying in a hotel, presumably in case of sexual opportunities. He worked hard at establishing himself as a contributor to village life in Abinger, too, collaborating with composer Ralph Vaughan Williams on the Abinger Pageant in 1934. Forster also bought the wood adjoining West Hackhurst to prevent development. Characteristically, he encouraged the villagers to continue to walk through it and picnic within it.

The Second World War affected Forster greatly, though he saw the necessity of fighting Hitler and helped out, in the sense that he happily incorporated elements of propaganda into book broadcasts for the BBC. But he was conflicted. As he had argued to Cecil Day-Lewis in October 1938, the Allies faced a choice: either to 'yield' to Nazism and be 'subdued', or else they could resist it, but in so doing, 'come to resemble them… and are subdued to them that way'. He was a diehard supporter of liberal democracy, but the title of his post-war collection of essays, *Two Cheers for Democracy*, points to reservations. He told Hilton Young in November 1939 that his support came 'because I am afraid to believe in anything else.' In case this sounded too weak, however, Forster added, 'history giving me, I submit, good reasons for such fear'. War at any time was ghastly; but technology had rendered it barbaric; it 'has moved from chivalry to chemicals,' he summarised in the plainspoken style that characterised his political essays for *Time and Tide*.

His readiness to broadcast propaganda may well surprise anyone recalling his famous dictum, itself from a 1939 broadcast, 'What I Believe': 'If I had to choose between betraying my country and betraying my friend, I hope I should have the guts to betray my country.' But the Second World War, he reasoned, was – unlike the First – 'a writers' and artists' war'; in opposing Nazism, Forster was clear that he was fighting as much for freedom of expression as for freedom at large. Aged eighty-seven, he wrote to tell Professor Wilfred Stone that he was proud to have written and broadcast 'a great deal of propaganda'; when the Germans came across it, he continued, 'I was put on their list for annihilation.' He was careful always to distinguish between the German population and their hideous government, though he also allowed, in 1941, that people's strong feelings might blind them to the need to distinguish in this way. 'Don't try to love them: you can't,' he wrote of the German people. 'You'll only strain yourself. But try to tolerate them.'

Forster found solidarity in the lunchtime piano concerts in the National Gallery, organised by Myra Hess. He was, though, pessimistic, repeatedly concluding that the war was lost. His old friend Florence Barger was bombed in London in September 1940; the Forsters invited her to stay at West Hackhurst for the next eighteen months. Evacuees soon filled Abinger, though it was subject to frequent attacks, given its proximity to London. Lily, meanwhile, needed a lot of care; she had acute arthritis and never left the house and garden. The running of both was effectively now entrusted to a single maid. In October, as he was writing a letter to Plomer from the house, Forster heard 'a bomber... overhead, on its way to all I love in London... it seems to me that the Germans have got our defences beat generally.' Also in 1940 he wrote to Isherwood, 'I am sure there is hope, but want someone else to do the hoping.' Isherwood responded by sending food parcels from the land of plenty. Forster's despair paradoxically emboldened him, however. On matters he considered essential, he was no pushover. Isherwood described him to others as 'immensely, superhumanly strong'. What he could not do, progressively, was commit himself to writing books. In 1933, he told Isherwood of his monograph study of Dickinson, 'It's so long since I've written a book that it feels like opening a tomb.'

Forster had aged quickly. This was exacerbated by being close to his mother and her conservative ways for so many decades. At thirty-six, he told Florence Barger, 'I am getting awfully revolutionary in my old age.' 'What is old age like?' he had already asked at thirty-two. Fate – cruelly, perhaps – gave him another sixty years to find out. A year earlier he had lamented the intrusion of the 'telephone and the bicycle, which have between them done so much to disintegrate family life'. Revealingly, when discussing a novel of Hugh Walpole's, he told the author in respect of characterisation and age that he had portrayed one middle-aged male character as too young, 'His development is just what one might expect in the 20's... though men may keep buoyancy, freshness & charm, they *must* lose adaptability.' That stressed '*must*' suggests a need to find others maturing in life at least as concretely as Morgan felt he was himself.

By 1937, he could write, 'I feel I can't adapt myself anymore'; 'I am sorry to have lived into these 1930s... because I am not equipped to understand them.' The war saw him looking after Lily throughout her decline; it is unsurprising that mortality was on his mind. He thought himself 'awfully indifferent to my own death', as he wrote to Buckingham in 1943, 'but easily upset when people I love are threatened.' In 1945 – after Lily's death, he confessed, 'I partly died when my mother did, and must smell sometimes of the grave.' Even then, he had another quarter of a century to go. Christopher Isherwood, quintessentially and eternally boyish in outlook, must have tired of his correspondent's nannyish disposition, and in the 1950s and 1960s what had been a fulsome correspondence dwindled. Forster could find little of merit in anything contemporary, including the unstoppable cultural dominance of film. Isherwood, meanwhile, was working on cinematic projects in Hollywood – in 1948, seeking to entice Forster into agreeing to a movie based on *A Passage to India*. He would not consider it.

Lily died in March 1945, after falling twice out of the bed to which she had been confined. Florence Barger watched as Forster tended to his dying mother, paying tribute to 'all the love and tenderness' he showed. 'You must expect to find me a bit altered,' he warned Buckingham, immediately afterwards. But he adopted a position beyond stoic to others, telling Ackerley, 'My mouldy mother, as you once called her, is dead, and I now expect to start mouldering myself.' Part of him had always succumbed to their dependent relationship. He would always find a phone on reaching a destination to assure Lily he had arrived safely. Another side, however, felt release – release, above all, from her scrutiny and from the duties of caring. He had tended to use certain trusted friends to vent his frustrations to. Forster wrote to Ackerley in 1938, 'She has been intermittently tiresome for the last 30 years, cramped and warped my genius, hindered my career, blocked and buggered up my house and boycotted my beloved,' by which he meant Buckingham. He often reacted coolly to death, however. When Barger died in 1954, he was sad, but confessed only, 'I have suddenly wanted to think and look at warm obscenities.' In similar vein, late in life Forster spent more and more time reading explicit gay literature, with an evident taste for happy endings in the more populist novels. He even imported more or less compromising material, once flashing an American magazine full of male nudes. He and Ackerley visited a London gay-friendly coffeehouse entitled 'The Mousehole', even though its ambience was 'very sad'; they almost got arrested once when it was raided.

The lease on West Hackhurst had already expired, but the house's owners, the Farrers, had allowed the Forsters to stay, given Lily's frailty. Once she had died, however, Forster himself needed new accommodation; the Farrers had other ambitions for the house. He never forgave what he considered their high-handedness, though they were quite within their rights. He would write to John Meade in 1959 that he no longer missed West Hackhurst, as to live there alone would have been unpleasant. Nevertheless, 'I still feel angry with those Farrers who turned me out of a house my father built.'

A solution came readily. King's had elected him a Supernumerary Fellow between 1927 and 1933. George Rylands, a friend, now readily persuaded the college to make Forster an Honorary Fellow. He had a good study in King's, part of Wedd's old rooms, but lived with a longstanding friend and King's don, Patrick Wilkinson, in two spare rooms in 3 Trumpington Street

– 'a refuge', Wilkinson would refer to it in 1969, 'from the flattering but exhausting attentions of the "Forster industry".' (For similar reasons, in college, Forster refused the offer of a telephone.) Excess furnishings from Abinger were sold off; in April 1945, Morgan could report to William Plomer that he had been ripping up 'hundreds of letters in which one woman writes to another about the ill health of a third'. After seven years, when the Wilkinsons moved, Forster moved into the college itself. He retained a few pieces of furniture of sentimental importance, especially an oval walnut dining table which had belonged to Marianne Thornton. But he could not feel at home thus, complaining when he moved in that 'I see my furniture everywhere, my home nowhere.'

Still, this was the sort of generosity only the Oxford and Cambridge colleges could extend to gifted alumni in those days – knowing, naturally, that the association reflected credit back upon the institution. In October 1946 Forster spent his first night in Cambridge, finding that 'if I am to live that sort of life things couldn't be nicer.' He never ceased to be grateful. In 1952, responding to a toast to the college during 'Founders Feast', he wryly noted his good fortune: 'I hold no College office; I attend no committee; I sit on no body, however solid, not even on the Annual Congregation; I co-opt not, neither am I co-opted; I teach not, neither do I think, and even the glory in which I am now arrayed was borrowed from another College for the occasion.'

Yet the arrangement was apt in other ways. Forster wrote of 'Goldie' Dickinson that 'by the end of his life he had become so wise that he was able to learn from the young.' Forster similarly was never aloof before the undergraduates and involved himself deeply in college life, attending talks, performances, drama productions, and turning up routinely to join undergraduates for tea. In turn they regarded him as a peer, since, as Plomer commented, 'one did not think of him in terms of age.' Not everybody was impressed. Novelist-to-be Simon Raven arrived at King's to find Forster 'bone idle... for ever pottering from nowhere in particular to nowhere else'.

October 1945 saw Forster embark on his final visit to India, for a conference organised by PEN in Jaipur. During the war, Forster had sympathised with the imprisoned nationalist leader Jayah Prakash Narayan, and was thrilled at the prospective emergence of an independent state, which the British granted on 15th August 1947. But he found the political turmoil had sapped Indians of their cultural breadth and complained, 'Literature, in their view, should expound or inspire a political creed.' The people, he felt, were markedly less well-educated. Yet, paradoxically, he became a hero to India precisely because of what he had written. K. Natwar-Singh has underlined how *A Passage to India* had, for natives, swept away the embarrassing burden of being known to Westerners by way of Rudyard Kipling's images of orientalist superiority. This was particularly true of Kipling's verse, which Forster disliked strongly. He was not alone. Orwell found Kipling's writings 'morally offensive and aesthetically disgusting'. It was 'all that tosh about the white man's burden and the stiff upper lip which made the sahibs at Poona and Cheltenham feel so pukka', as Natwar-Singh phrased it in 1969. Forster grew tired of the acclaim, however, writing to Buckingham, 'The penalty of greatness is powerlessness, and I am seldom able to see or do what I want.' Still, he decided, 'I wanted to be with Indians, and was, and that is a very little step in the right direction.' He saw Delhi, Bombay, 'dreadful' Calcutta, but also took time in Hyderabad to meet old friends. There were side trips to Ajanta's Buddhist frescoed caves, and to Santiniketan ('The Home of Peace'), inspiration to the esteemed Bengali mystic poet Rabindranath Tagore, who had been acclaimed in Britain before his death in 1941. Both Masood and Bapu Sahib, the Maharajah of Dewas Senior, however, had died in 1937.

In April 1947, Forster saw the United States of America for the first time. He was increasingly wary of long-haul travel, and rarely ever flew, but made the journey aged sixty-eight following an invitation from Harvard University to lecture at a Symposium on Music, but above all to see a young actor, William Roerick, who had served in the US Army in England in 1943, met Forster through Isherwood and encouraged the visit, suggesting that Forster go out a month before his Harvard duties to see something of the country. Forster saw his publishers in New York, where he began his stay. Though Roerick arranged for his mother to accommodate Forster, she was perturbed by his habit of covering fully half of his bed with books, letters, glasses, and even fruit, so that she could not properly make it up. Forster and Roerick then spent some time in the rural Berkshires, Western Massachusetts, going over the address he was to give, before Forster headed on alone. He made a special visit to a small college in upstate New York, Hamilton, which had adopted the village school in Abinger after the war, providing it with books, stationery and more. Forster turned up to show his gratitude.

He then made for the Grand Canyon by plane, a mode of transport he had been initiated into in Alexandria in 1918. He descended on mule back, thus entitling him to membership of the 'Bum Bumpers Club', and was stunned by its natural beauty. Forster went on to Los Angeles, where he saw Isherwood, and went north for San Francisco, the Golden Gate Bridge and the Yosemite Valley before returning by train (via Chicago) – first to New York, where he spent time in the Greenwich Village apartment of celebrated gay painter Paul Cadmus, who had sent Forster a fan letter years earlier. Cadmus introduced him to a young writer friend, Donald Windham, whom he liked and whose works he supported. He also went to the theatre, capturing the legendary Broadway performer Ethel Merman in *Annie Get Your Gun*, and got to know Lionel Trilling, who had so boosted his reputation stateside with his 1944 study of Forster's novels, and his wife Diana. He headed south to the federal capital, where he was privileged to be given a tour of the collected loot of art from Nazi Germany, removed from a salt mine by the American Army and brought back for safekeeping. Finally, he went back to Tyringham in the Berkshires, where Roerick put him up at his own dilapidated house called 'Lost Farm'. Here Forster was interviewed by *The New Yorker*, and admitted to being 'a frightful old bore'. Roerick recalled Forster's habit of conducting small talk wherever he went, listening carefully to the stories of farm women, taking advice from waitresses on what not to order and comparing subway maps with a train conductor. Forster grew convinced that, where the English might display habitual manners, these were a duty rather than true manifestations of politeness. He burst into laughter when one friend countered his attempt to handle a restaurant bill by insisting, 'Drop dead, Forster, I'm paying this!' In fact, he was displaying something characteristic in himself, but rare in others of whatever nationality. As Plomer put it, Forster was 'a rare specialist in detecting and bringing out the qualities of "ordinary" persons, and in making them feel they mattered to him'.

He left America on 12th July 1947 as he had found it – full of 'charm and friendliness', just the opposite of 'malnourished, disgruntled England'. In 1948 in Cambridge he fell into a deep depression caused by Buckingham's perceived neglect; his diary notes that he was 'tired of people and personal relationships... I want to see no one.' It was small wonder that in May 1949, he visited America again, this time taking Buckingham along. He lectured at the Academy of Art and Letters on 'Art for Art's Sake', an oddly uncongenial subject for Forster. They kept to the East Coast, mostly visiting people Forster knew.

Between 1949 and 1951, Forster collaborated with Benjamin Britten, co-writing the libretto for the opera *Billy Budd* with Eric Crozier; it was based on the homoerotic short story by Herman Melville. Britten and Crozier found Forster a congenial collaborator. The composer noted his 'deep perception, quick wit, tireless energy... and, in spite of his doubts ("I am not creative any longer") his consistent inspiration.' Forster felt a sympathy with Melville, who in the tale had, he felt, failed in a way that he himself had failed – to capture 'the ordinary lovable (and hateable [sic]) human beings connected with immensities through the tricks of art. Billy *is* our Saviour, yet he is Billy, not Christ' (letter to Britten, 20th December 1948). He wrote to Trilling, who had studied Melville's story extensively, asking pointed questions. Forster wondered too at what indeed was a rare distinction of the opera: it had only male parts. *Billy Budd* was a huge success on its first performance at the Royal Opera House on 1st December 1951.

Forster was, as ever, happy to start new epistolary friendships. He had enjoyed Frank Sargeson's novel *I Saw in My Dream* (1949), and wrote to the New Zealand novelist telling him so. The same year, 1949, he refused a knighthood, though in 1953 he accepted the Companion of Honour, and in 1969, he received the Order of Merit. In 1953, he wrote to Nellie Whichelo, one of his aunts, that the (new) Queen, 'quite an ickle thing', had been delightful – 'much better at the chat' than he himself. That year, he went on holiday to Portugal with the young P.N. ('Nick') Furbank, to whom he would eventually entrust the task of writing his biography. He liked the 'slow and rather unattractive' Portuguese. If Forster was slowing up, it was not by much. Early 1953 saw him in France, touring with Bill Roerick and a friend, Tom Coley. In April 1958, he took Bob and May Buckingham on a cruise to Greece and Istanbul, by way of Venice.

Throughout the 1960s, Forster received royalties on a hugely successful stage adaptation of *A Passage to India* undertaken by Santha Rama Rau on several continents. Although in 1948 he had dismissed a suggested cinema adaptation out of hand, throughout the 1950s and 1960s, the authoress and others would return to the possibility in vain. A letter to her dated 20th July 1967 pithily states, 'I didn't and I don't want *A Passage* filmed. I am so sorry.' (Forster regularly used the word 'barbarians' to describe those involved in Hollywood cinema.) Likewise he refused an approach to film *A Room with a View* when in America in 1947. Fox had offered him $25,000; on his refusal, they improved the offer. Perversely, it was Isherwood's account of the farcical filming of 1934's *Little Friend*, which he had co-scripted, in the novel *Prater Violet* (1945) that convinced Forster to say no. He had concluded that 'Nothing would have survived of the original except my name, and if I had tried to control the production I should have broken my heart at Hollywood, besides spending my life there.'

Forster faced calamity after calamity in the 1960s. Florence Barger died in 1960 – an upset, despite her being 'as if dead for months'. He had a serious heart attack himself in 1962. Numerous strokes followed. After the most serious, in 1966, Forster could barely read or write, as his eyesight was impaired. Little substantial correspondence survives thereafter. In any case, his sense of slowing up intellectually hit Forster much sooner; his *Commonplace Book* entry for 31st January 1961 was entitled 'Going to Bits'. It was 'not tragic, not mortal disintegration, only a central weakness which prevents me from concentrating or settling down'. Sure enough, that April, he broke his wrist on the doorway of Ackerley's Putney flat, and suffered badly from shock. He was rescued by Buckingham, and returned to Cambridge where he spent several nights in hospital. Still, his constitution was infinitely stronger than Lily had ever imagined, and he would survive the decade – infrequently 'prone to senile lechery', he informed Ackerley, but resigned to dealing with it through his 'licentious scribblings'. Whenever he was seriously unwell, he was welcomed by the Buckinghams in Coventry.

Forster lived so long that, inevitably, he outlived many younger writers whose careers he had promoted, such as Joe Ackerley, who died in 1967. Their late dealings had been awkward. Ackerley, driven by dire financial need, had been negotiating with the University of Texas over the possible sale of his cache of Forster letters – full, of course, of what struck Forster as compromising material. Ackerley knew Forster had the means to buy the letters; for whatever reason, he rejected the possibility of this, saying, 'Nor do I want them in his hands... For I should never get them back again, and I have both a personal and a posterity interest in them.' It may seem that Ackerley rewarded Forster poorly for his ongoing generosity; the latter routinely wrote his friend cheques. Still, Forster had a patrician attitude to generosity, attaching conditions to those cheques, which Ackerley did not always abide by. Told by Forster to return to the Far East, Ackerley instead blew his windfall by dining out in London.

In 1961, Forster decided he had at least £1,000 that he wanted to give to charities. He consulted with Plomer, as to which struggling young writers might discreetly be helped. He also wanted to support what was then called the Homosexual Law Reform Society, an organisation that would eventually successfully campaign for the (partial) decriminalisation of male homosexual offences in 1967. Forster asked Plomer if he knew whether the Society was 'efficient' or 'influential'. Giving away funds became part of Forster's daily life. Nevertheless, by the late 1960s, he had accumulated the truly immense sum of £25,000 in his current account.

By 1968, Nick Furbank had embarked on gathering material for his biography, with Forster's help. Oliver Stallybrass gathered a set of reminiscences in *Aspects of E.M. Forster* to coincide with his ninetieth birthday, duly published in 1969. Forster was still taking excursions in his last years, including one summer to the Aldeburgh Festival, launched by Benjamin Britten and Peter Pears and run annually in the Suffolk fishing village. Little is known of how unwell he was precisely when he died – on 7th June 1970 in Coventry, at the Buckinghams'. Forster had asked to be cremated; his ashes were scattered over their garden.

He had never seriously considered returning to the Christian faith he had had as a child. But to the end he had been intrigued by its intricacies and consequences. In 1948 he wrote to Benjamin Britten that he loved 'the tenderness and pity and love' of Christianity; its advocates, he thought, were 'interfering and weepy' (they thus resembled his mother). The 1958 cruise to Greece had revived Forster's interest in ancient beliefs; writing during it, he suggested to Eric Fletcher that the Ancients did well not to get 'bogged down in Original Sin. I don't exactly dislike Christianity, but it is such a relief to get away into a world that isn't coloured by it.'

He died, effectively, as the humanist he had always been as an adult. The humanist, Forster had argued in an essay on André Gide, 'has four leading characteristics – curiosity, a free mind, belief in good taste, and belief in the human race'. Humanism encouraged Forster to downplay any possibility of trauma attending 'the hour of death', as he noted in an address given to the Cambridge Humanist Society (of which he was President) in 1959: death, he added 'may scare, it may hurt, it probably ends the individual, but in comparison to the hours when a man is alive, the hour of death is almost negligible'.

He may always have felt he had little in common with Henry James. But both authors, arguably, approached the afterlife primarily by writing for posterity, the atheist or agnostic's traditional aim at eternal life. As Forster had written to Isherwood in 1937 on hearing of the fatal accident which occurred to a friend, Peter Burra, whilst flying, 'Death turns the dead person into something worse than nothing – something *deflecting* – where all one's affection for him or criticism of him becomes false. The most satisfactory dead are those who have published books.'

Afterlife

Forster's reputation today stands – as it did in the latter half of his life – chiefly upon *A Passage to India* and its 'moral intelligence' (Plomer's phrase). There are, naturally, however, many admirers of all the novels and stories. Indeed, each offers us something. By 1934, Forster himself felt that the Indian novel 'stands', while thinking that the 'fissures' in the earlier fictions were 'considerable'. In 1937 he noted to Isherwood the 'amazing luck' that his best book was his most popular one 'and the one most likely to do good'. His writings as a critic were founded on an often rather invisible confidence; he felt clear, for instance, that his work was superior to that of George Eliot, whom he thought talented as a 'moralist' but not exactly a novelist. His status as a truly modern great novelist was reinforced single-handedly by Lionel Trilling, in his influential monograph of 1944. Forster's virtues, Trilling argued, were modern ones – suited to the age, in a sense, as they were secular and humanistic: 'He is content with the human possibility and content with its limitations.'

The publication of *Maurice* in 1971 proved somewhat awkward for Forster's legacy. Cyril Connolly put it best, arguing that, though the theme was entirely timely, the manner of Forster's style, and the dialogue in the book, made it seem irrelevant: 'The element of dating is fatal, like foxing on a book... We can make allowances for what dates if it was once contemporary, even as the foxed pages were once immaculate, but there's something artificial where a book is born dated.' *Maurice* widened the scope of Forster's oeuvre – but we should ask whether it deepened his literary achievement. The appended note suggests the author's own view: that changes in society and the law had, paradoxically, rendered the book historical in too many ways; and not merely quaint-historical, in the manner, perhaps of Evelyn Waugh's *Brideshead Revisited* (1945). By 1971, gay themes were coming in, but agony and self-agonising were out of style.

The Life to Come and Other Stories (1972) is another difficult book. Though there were jewels, such as the title story and a true work of 'Indian Summer' genius entitled 'The Other Boat' (1957), there were also pieces offering less convincing, period-bound or somewhat laboured exchanges – sexual and otherwise. Perversely, what had sharpened *A Passage to India* – Forster's pronounced liberal politics, and his sense of the universal significance of the mores and cultural values he portrayed – was largely missing when he handled homosexual themes in fiction. Regarding his own sexuality, Forster never desired to take secrets to the grave: 'But when I die and they write my life, they can say everything,' he wrote to T.E. Lawrence in 1928. Equally, one properly hesitates to make too much of Forster's shortcomings in fiction, as the author himself pushed self-deprecation to extreme limits.

1977 saw the *Times Literary Supplement* asking writers who they felt had an inflated literary reputation; two respondents cited Forster, both surprisingly: Angus Wilson, author of a succession of gay-themed novels from the 1950s to the 1980s; and Anthony Powell, author of the *A Dance to the Music of Time* sequence, more a stylistic peer. Wilson had attended an eightieth birthday lunch for Forster at King's, and they had corresponded. The same year, Noel Annan wrote in *The Listener* that Forster had had the bad luck to have prophesied and argued for causes that became acceptable; hence, 'one of the reasons he no longer speaks to us is that we listened and followed his advice.'

This is overly dismissive and makes little sense today. A spate of film adaptations throughout the 1980s brought Forster a new readership, as well as renewed critical attention and acclaim. Lay readers have continued to appreciate what Elizabeth Bowen termed his 'lucidity'. Bowen, as a young girl, had grown attuned to his sense of irony, an 'irony partly holding mockery in curb' and so quintessentially proper and Edwardian in feel. He could make ordinary speech feel unpredictable and momentous; to her, he was 'the master dialogue-writer of our century'. Bowen noted the centrality of passion to most of Forster's characters. The right or wrong placing of a kiss, for one thing, is a dominant plot concern in both *A Room with a View* and *Howards End*. But there are passions other than the sexual, such as Leonard Bast's for self-improvement.

Christopher Isherwood paid a tribute to Forster, the 'anti-heroic hero', in *Down There on a Visit* in 1962: 'While the others tell their followers to be ready to die, he advises us to live as if we were immortal.' Forster's tangible influence on gay male literary style has been immense – from Isherwood's own embrace of 'tea-tabling' to the powerful, popular works of David Leavitt, America's foremost Forster standard bearer. Many of Leavitt's novels and stories contain references, subtle and overt, to Forsterian plots, characters, books and literary stylistics. With 2008's *The Indian Clerk*, Leavitt effectively wrote a novel Forster could have written (and at whose margins he stands) – the story of a mathematician academic in Cambridge, G.H. Hardy, who is contacted by an Indian prodigy in the same field, Srinivasa Ramanujan, in 1913.

Forster's life poses a number of problems. Chief of these must be that so much of it – especially after 1924's *A Passage to India* – must primarily be read for its own interest. Fortunately, almost all of it is very fascinating. His faith in Furbank portraying him fairly in the biography to be written after his death was fully rewarded; further details, inevitably, have become known since Furbank's late-seventies volumes, but nothing has challenged the wide arc of achievement in them, or the emphases placed on particular events and works.

Conversely, *Passage* aside, the novels on which Forster's reputation is based, largely – and always indirectly – drew on a relatively small body of experience, all over by his thirtieth birthday. Forster's own attitude to literary biography was perplexing, since he thought himself free of interest in other writers' lives, and cautioned against bringing it into play when reading their works: 'Don't bother about reconciling the statements in my books with my conduct at the table,' he told T.E. Lawrence in 1927. But his own judgments only rarely chimed with this opinion. His respect for Christopher Isherwood's English novels had been fulsome – especially in respect of *The Memorial* (1932), for example; Isherwood had fully fictionalised his experiences and concerns. But in response to Isherwood's American novels – which played with aspects of the memoir form, and may consequently be thought of as 'autofictions', Forster could only muster up tepid responses. He noted to his friend 'disappointments and difficulties' with *The World in the Evening* (1954). To *Down There on a Visit* (1962), he reacted abruptly: 'I didn't come off with your book'; 'I didn't want Christopher or his variants to guide me through a book by you any more… I want a yarn less conditioned by him. I had other reservations…'

It was more characteristic – whatever his stated opinions – for Forster to conflate literary and personal sensibilities – the writer, that is, and the man (or, less commonly, woman). By 1962, he could summarise the way his and Isherwood's paths had diverged boldly, 'There is a part of me, of my literary and personal character, which is very far from what you are and stand for… I don't mean by this that I am apologising for myself or even for the book [of Isherwood's].' As he had argued as an undergraduate student of the poet Dryden, 'As was his character, so too are his poems.' Forster's privileging of empathetic reading of literature, and of an essentially biographically informed view of authors and their works, produces some odd notes in his critical writings, but also the occasional bull's eye. In 1931, Forster dispatched Dryden with the words, 'The very middle of the man is dead.' He could be prey to impressionistic judgments. Of the fiction of George Orwell, whom he knew and had worked for, Forster noted in 1942, 'He is strange and I dislike something in what he writes without being able to chase it into daylight.' Moreover, where Forster was genuinely ambivalent concerning others' personal qualities, the rhetorical consequences could be shattering. A year after Virginia Woolf's suicide, he wrote, 'I can never get clear in my mind as to whether she was right or wrong to go: at any rate she gave us something to think about.'

Such deliberations on human character were, fundamentally, at odds with Forster's wider view of human nature. This had been informed by readings in Samuel Butler and works relating to Eastern spiritualism. Paraphrasing Butler, Forster once argued, 'We are none of us personalities but bundles of instincts.' At other times, he oscillated back to accepting the separation between authorial character and literary artefact. Of Walter Pater's personality, Forster argued that it 'scarcely prepares us for the greatness of his books'. He disliked others' biographical criticism greatly. One victim was Peter Quennell, of whose 1949 study of John Ruskin, Forster wrote, 'Not being all that weak-minded, I am not put off *The Stones of Venice* by being told that Ruskin tossed himself off, but some readers might be deflected or disgusted... and not read him in consequence.'

Above all, he suspected Oscar Wilde's aestheticist insistence on the autonomy of Art, over or against human life. He repeatedly accused Wilde of triviality, and in 1921 perfunctorily announced without further elaboration, 'However much we condemn the way in which Wilde was treated as a man, we do not think him great as a writer.' In 1931's lecture 'The Creator as Critic', he argued rather differently: that Wilde was 'a mixture of the shoddy and the fine'. Once again, though, he did not elaborate – invariably Forster's way of indicating a literary talent too slight to elaborate on. Given the two writers' distinct but overlapping significance to our own debates concerning sexual identity, racial politics, post-colonial cultures, the stand-off between liberal ethics and more radical political positions, it is a curious and compelling fact that – to Forster at least – he and Wilde – today both undisputed gay literary icons and primary influences upon the many manifestations of gay culture that have succeeded them – had little to say to one another.

When privately teased over his failure to write more fiction, Forster sometimes countered that the only thing he still wanted to say was: 'love'. This, he argued, if repeated incessantly, would prove repetitious. The notorious epigraph to *Howards End* – 'Only connect' – and the close friendship of Aziz and Fielding in *A Passage to India* alike remain worthy illustrations of the sincerity of Forster's injunction, however. His ambition in life, he once conceded, was to be able to remain capable of embracing new people and new ideas until he died: 'I hope that I shall be able to fall in love with a new idea on my death-bed,' he told Roerick.

Ironically, of obituaries to Forster, the most moving published in 1970 came from the already dead Ackerley. It was written in 1967 for *The Observer*'s future use. Ackerley stated, 'In so far as it is possible for any human being to be both wise and worldly wise, to be selfless in any material sense, to have no envy, jealousy, vanity, conceit, to contain no malice, no hatred (though he had anger), to be always reliable, considerate, generous, never cheap, Morgan came as close to that as can be got.' Morality and courtesy may seem rather abstract qualities to stress at the end of a literary life. But Forster's generosity throughout his broad engagement with literature, culture, politics, philosophy and art is as significant a measure of and tribute to the man as the six fine novels he wrote and the impressive further writings. The most apt final word comes from his contribution to a Third Programme series encouraging people to 'sound off', entitled

'I Speak for Myself', aired in 1949. Forster characteristically opened his slot by noting that the very idea of speaking for oneself 'means... the power to realise that other people also speak'.

Chronological List of Works

1905 *Where Angels Fear to Tread*
1907 *The Longest Journey*
1908 *A Room with a View*
1910 *Howards End*
1911 *The Celestial Omnibus*
1922 *Alexandria: a History and a Guide*
1923 *Pharos and Pharillon*
1924 *A Passage to India*
1927 *Aspects of the Novel*
1928 *The Eternal Moment*
1934 *Goldsworthy Lowes Dickinson*
1936 *Abinger Harvest*
1947 *Collected Short Stories*
1951 *Two Cheers for Democracy*
(with Eric Crozier) *Billy Budd*
1953 *The Hill of Devi*
1956 *Marianne Thornton*

Posthumous publications

1971 *Maurice*
1972 *The Life to Come and Other Stories*
1980 *Arctic Summer and other fiction*
1983 *Selected Letters, volume one 1879–1920*
1985 *Selected Letters, volume two 1921–1970*
1988 *Commonplace Book*
2008 *The BBC Talks of E M Forster, 19291960*
The Creator as Critic and Other Writings by E M Forster
(with Christopher Isherwood) *Letters between Forster and Isherwood on Homosexuality and Literature*

Bibliography

The most comprehensive life to date remains the one approved by Forster himself in his last years, by P.N. Furbank. Mary Lago's 'literary life' interweaves readings of the novels with biographical details. Oliver Stallybrass's collection of reminiscences, *Aspects of E.M. Forster*, remains useful, as do the two selections of Forster's correspondence. This book is the first to benefit from three important recent additions to Forster's oeuvre: Jeffrey Heath's bountiful edition of uncollected writings, *The Creator as Critic*; Lago, Hughes et al's substantial edition of broadcasts for the BBC; and the selected letters of Forster and Isherwood, edited by Zeikowitz. Much of the quotation from Forster's correspondence is drawn from the two volumes of selected letters of E.M Forster, edited by Lago and Furbank. Almost all of the material in these books, however, forms part of the E.M. Forster Archive at Kings College, Cambridge.

The following works have all been consulted:

J.R. Ackerley, *E.M. Forster: a Portrait* (London, 1970)

Stephen D. Adams, *The Homosexual as Hero in Contemporary Fiction* (New York, 1980)

Peter Alexander, *William Plomer: a Biography* (Oxford, 1989)

P. Bakshi, *Distant Desire: Homoerotic Codes and the Subversion of the English Novel in E.M. Forster's Fiction* (New York, 1996)

Nicola Beauman, *Morgan: a Biography of E.M. Forster* (London, 1993)

J.B. Beer, *The Achievement of E.M. Forster* (London, 1962)

Gordon Bowker, 'Radio Reviews', *Times Literary Supplement* (19th September 2008)

Malcolm Bradbury (ed.), *Forster: a Collection of Critical Essays* (London, 1966)

David Bradshaw (ed.), *The Cambridge Companion to E.M. Forster* (Cambridge, 2007)

Joseph Bristow, *Effeminate England: Homoerotic Writing after 1885* (New York/London, 1995)

Les Brookes, *Gay Male Fiction Since Stonewall: Ideology, Conflict and Aesthetics* (London/New York, 2009)

Richard Canning, 'Tomb with a View', *Worldwide Gay and Lesbian Review* (March–April, 2009)
John Colmer, *E.M. Forster: the Personal Voice* (London, 1975)
Antony Copley, *A Spiritual Bloomsbury: Hinduism and Homosexuality in the Lives and Writings of Edward Carpenter, E.M. Forster and Christopher Isherwood* (Lanham, MD, 2006)
Frederick Crews, *E.M. Forster: the Perils of Humanism* (London, 1962)
Richard Cronin, *Imagining India* (London: 1989)
Harry Daley, *This Small Cloud: a Personal Memoir* (London, 1986)
Goldsworthy Lowes Dickinson, *Autobiography* (London, 1973)
Mike Edwards, *E.M. Forster: the Novels* (London, 2001)
John Fletcher, 'Forster's Self-Erasure: *Maurice* and the Scene of Masculine Love', in Joseph Bristow (ed.), *Sexual Sameness: Textual Differences in Lesbian and Gay Writing* (London / New York, 1992)
E.M. Forster, *Abinger Harvest* (London, 1936)
E.M. Forster, *Alexandria: a History and a Guide* (London, 1986; originally 1922), edited by Michael Haag
E.M. Forster, *Arctic Summer and other fiction* (London, 1980)
E.M. Forster, *Aspects of the Novel* (London, 1990; originally 1927), edited by Oliver Stallybrass
E.M. Forster, *The BBC Talks of E. M. Forster, 1929–1960* (Columbia / London, 2008), edited by Mary Lago, Linda K. Hughes and Elizabeth Macleod Walls
E.M. Forster, *Commonplace Book* (Aldershot, 1988), edited by Philip Gardner
E.M. Forster, *The Creator as Critic and Other Writings by E.M. Forster* (Toronto: 2008), edited by Jeffrey M. Heath
E.M. Forster, *Pharos and Pharillon* (London, 1986; originally 1923), edited by Michael Haag
E.M. Forster, *Selected Letters, volume one 1879–1920* (London, 1983), edited by Mary Lago and P.N. Furbank
E.M. Forster, *Selected Letters, volume two 1921–1970* (Cambridge, MA, 1985), edited by Mary Lago and P.N. Furbank
E.M. Forster, *Two Cheers for Democracy* (London, 1951)
E.M. Forster and Christopher Isherwood, *Letters between Forster and Isherwood on Homosexuality and Literature* (New York / Basingstoke, 2008), edited by Richard Zeikowitz
P.N. Furbank, *E.M. Forster: a Life* (London, 1979; vol.1 first published 1977; vol.2 first published 1978)
Philip Gardner (ed.), *E.M. Forster: the Critical Heritage* (London, 1973)
Michael Haag, *Alexandria: City of Memory* (New Haven / London, 2004)
Judith Scherer Herz, *The Short Narratives of E.M. Forster* (London, 1988)
Judith Scherer Herz and Robert K. Martin (eds.), *E.M. Forster: Centenary Revaluations* (Toronto, 1982)
Christopher Isherwood, *Christopher and His Kind, 1929–39* (London, 1977)

J.K. Johnstone, *The Bloomsbury Group* (London, 1954)
Frank Kermode, 'Fiction and E.M. Forster', *London Review of Books* (10th May 2007)
Frank Kermode, 'Sly Digs', *London Review of Books* (25th September 2008)
John Maynard Keynes, *Two Memoirs* (London, 1949)
Francis King, *E.M. Forster and His World* (London, 1978; rev. ed. 1988)
B.J. Kirkpatrick, *A Bibliography of E.M. Forster* (Oxford, 1985; rev. ed.)
Mary Lago, *E.M. Forster: a Literary Life* (London/New York, 1995)
Hermione Lee, *Virginia Woolf* (London, 1996)
Robert Liddell, *Cavafy* (London, 1974)
Rose Macaulay, *The Writings of E. M. Forster* (London, 1938)
Robert K. Martin and George Piggsford (eds.), *Queer Forster* (Chicago, 1997)
Arthur Martland, *E.M. Forster: Passion and Prose* (London, 1997)
Frederick McDowell, *E.M. Forster: an Annotated Bibliography of Writings about Him* (London, 1976)
David Medalie, *E.M. Forster's Modernism* (London, 2002)
K. Natwar-Singh, *E.M. Forster: a Tribute* (New York, 1964)
Norman Page, *E.M. Forster's Posthumous Fiction* (Victoria, B.C, 1977)
Peter Parker, *Isherwood* (London, 2004)
Jane Lagoudis Pinchin, *Alexandria Still: Forster, Durrell and Cavafy* (Princeton, NJ/London, 1992)
William Plomer, *At Home* (London, 1958)
William Plomer, *Autobiography* (London, 1975)
Santha Rama Rau, *A Passage to India: a Play from the Novel by E.M. Forster* (London, 1960)
Sheila Rowbotham, *Edward Carpenter: a Life of Liberty and Love* (London, 2008)
Nicholas Royle, *E.M. Forster (Writers and their Work)* (London, 1999)
Mohammed Shaheen, *E.M. Forster and the Politics of Imperialism* (London, 2004)
Graham Smith, *Light that Dances in the Mind: Photographs and Memory in the Writings of E.M. Forster and His Contemporaries* (New York/Oxford, 2007)
Oliver Stallybrass (ed.), *Aspects of E.M. Forster* (London, 1969)
Wilfred Stone, *The Cave and the Mountain* (Stanford/Oxford, 1966)
Claude Summers, *E.M. Forster* (New York, 1983)
Claude Summers, *E.M. Forster: a Guide to Research* (New York, 1991)
Claude Summers, *Gay Fictions: Wilde to Stonewall* (New York, 1990)
Jeremy Tambling (ed.), *E.M. Forster: Contemporary Critical Essays* (London, 1995)
G.H. Thomson, *The Fiction of E.M. Forster* (London, 1967)
Lionel Trilling, *E.M. Forster: a Study* (London, 1944)
Rex Warner, *E.M. Forster* (London, 1950)
Alan Wilde, *Art and Order: a Study of E.M. Forster* (New York, 1964)
Alan Wilde (ed.), *Critical Essays on E.M. Forster* (Boston, 1985)

Acknowledgments

All passages from E.M. Forster's published and unpublished writings are within the copyright the Provost and Scholars of King's College, Cambridge, the executors of the E.M. Forster Estate. I am extremely grateful for their kind permission to draw on this material, and particularly want to thank Peter Jones, Librarian at Kings, and Elizabeth Haylett Clark at the Society of Authors for their help.

Biographical note

Richard Canning teaches in the School of English at the University of Sheffield. He has published widely in the field of gay literature. Publications include two volumes of conversations with gay novelists, *Gay Fiction Speaks* (New York, 2000) and *Hear Us Out* (New York, 2003); he is editor of the volumes of gay male fiction *Between Men* (New York, 2007) and *Between Men 2* (New York, 2009), as well as the AIDS fiction anthology *Vital Signs* (New York, 2007). Canning wrote Hesperus's *Brief Lives: Oscar Wilde* (London, 2008) and has been preparing a critical biography of Ronald Firbank, as well as an edition of Louis Couperus's *Fate (Noodlot)*.